THE SHOOTING SCRIPT®

ABOUT A BOY

SCREENPLAY BY
PETER HEDGES AND **CHRIS WEITZ** & **PAUL WEITZ**
BASED ON THE BOOK BY **NICK HORNBY**

INTRODUCTION BY
CHRIS WEITZ AND **PAUL WEITZ**

A Newmarket Shooting Script® Series Book
NEWMARKET PRESS • NEW YORK

FIRST EDITION

02 03 04 10 9 8 7 6 5 4 3 2 1

ISBN: 1-55704-571-2 (paperback)

Library of Congress Catalog-in-Publication Data is available upon request.

QUANTITY PURCHASES

Companies, professional groups, clubs, and other organizations may qualify for special terms when ordering quantities
of this title. For information, write to Special Sales, Newmarket Press, 18 East 48th Street, New York, NY 10017;
call (212) 832-3575 or 1-800-669-3903; FAX (212) 832-3629; or e-mail mailbox@newmarketpress.com.

Website: www.newmarketpress.com

Manufactured in the United States of America.

OTHER BOOKS IN THE NEWMARKET SHOOTING SCRIPT® SERIES INCLUDE:

The Age of Innocence: The Shooting Script	*Man on the Moon: The Shooting Script*
American Beauty: The Shooting Script	*The Matrix: The Shooting Script*
A Beautiful Mind: The Shooting Script	*Nurse Betty: The Shooting Script*
The Birdcage: The Shooting Script	*The People vs. Larry Flynt: The Shooting Script*
Blackhawk Down: The Shooting Script	*The Shawshank Redemption: The Shooting Script*
Cast Away: The Shooting Script	*Red Dragon: The Shooting Script*
Dead Man Walking: The Shooting Script	*Snatch: The Shooting Script*
Erin Brockovich: The Shooting Script	*Snow Falling on Cedars: The Shooting Script*
Gods and Monsters: The Shooting Script	*State and Main: The Shooting Script*
Gosford Park: The Shooting Script	*Traffic: The Shooting Script*
Human Nature: The Shooting Script	*The Truman Show: The Shooting Script*
The Ice Storm: The Shooting Script	*U-Turn: The Shooting Script*
Knight's Tale: The Shooting Script	

OTHER NEWMARKET PICTORIAL MOVIEBOOKS AND NEWMARKET INSIDER FILM BOOKS INCLUDE:

The Age of Innocence: A Portrait of the Film★	*The Jaws Log*
ALI: The Movie and The Man★	*Men in Black: The Script and the Story Behind the Film*★
Amistad: A Celebration of the Film by Steven Spielberg	*Neil Simon's Lost in Yonkers: The Illustrated Screenplay of the Film*★
The Art of The Matrix★	*Planet of The Apes: Re-imagined by Tim Burton*★
Bram Stoker's Dracula: The Film and the Legend★	*Saving Private Ryan: The Men, The Mission, The Movie*
Cradle Will Rock: The Movie and the Moment★	*The Sense and Sensibility Screenplay & Diaries*★
Crouching Tiger, Hidden Dragon: A Portrait of the Ang Lee Film★	*The Seven Years in Tibet Screenplay and Story*★
Dances with Wolves: The Illustrated Story of the Epic Film★	*Stuart Little: The Art, the Artists and the Story Behind the Amazing Movie*★
E.T. The Extra Terrestrial From Concept to Classic—The Illustrated Story of the Film and the Filmmakers	*Windtalkers: The Making of the Film About the Navajo Code Talkers of World War II*
Frida: Bringing Frida Kahlo's Life and Art to Film	
Gladiator: The Making of the Ridley Scott Epic Film	

★*Includes Screenplay*

CONTENTS

INTRODUCTION

BY CHRIS WEITZ AND PAUL WEITZ

We happened on *About a Boy* by accident. Nick Hornby's book was recommended to Chris as what is called, usually with a hint of disdain, a good read. It was that and more, as anybody who will take the time to read it will find out. That's a great part of Hornby's art—to be bouncy, populist, fun, even slick, while below the surface all sorts of points are making themselves felt. Chris called Paul and said, "We've got our Billy Wilder movie." We had been looking around awhile, in and outside of our own heads, for a Wilderesque film to make. By that word we meant, beyond the presumptuous implication of talented execution, a morally ambiguous or difficult subject that still had a popular element to it. We had swanned around town dropping Wilder's name every time a studio executive had asked us "what stuff we were interested in doing next," and were usually met with nods of recognition, real or feigned, but never with the right movie—or at least the right movie that somebody wanted *us* to direct. And here it was in the form of Hornby's book! All we had to do was snap up the rights and run with it.

As it happened, the rights had been bought three years earlier in a heated bidding war, which tells you something about our up-to-the-minute tracking of projects. The happy-go-lucky Will was in the hands of, of all people, Robert DeNiro. We made all speed to convince him and his partner Jane Rosenthal that we were the men for the job (or, to put it perhaps more appropriately, the boys for the job). After an initial meeting in which Paul unaccountably alienated Bob by making him feel he was out of touch for being unfamiliar with the historical novels of Patrick O'Brian, we got the job. God knows why. Later, Eric Fellner and Working Title joined in to risk their reputations on us as well.

A pre-existing script by a wonderful writer, Peter Hedges, had made Will an American expatriate. There was also a move afoot to transplant the book to the United States, an instinct that had borne fruit with *High Fidelity*, but we wanted to keep the movie in London. We had Mr. Hugh Grant in hand, or, as the term goes, "attached," and couldn't imagine anybody more suited to play the role. Besides which, he was clever and helpful with the script and a good boon companion. We felt that the film would benefit from the degree of specificity and sense of place and idiom that Hornby's writing hits. It was decided that the neighborhood of Clerkenwell, the old medieval center of London, would provide the right exteriors. It was only a stone's throw from Hornby's Holloway (though a galaxy away in the mind of a rabid Hornbyite) and the buildings, from Smithfield meat market to the more yuppistische kultur settings that Will fritters away his semi-life in, were resonant of a London that hadn't been post-carded to death.

Months of searching for a suitable Boy with the redoubtable casting agent Priscilla John turned up Nicholas Hoult, one of those rare unearthings you hope is not accompanied with a curse. When you get such a sweet-natured, clever, naturally talented child actor, you just thank your lucky stars and hope you don't turn him into a future bank robber. With Nicholas playing Marcus, we knew we had a personality strong enough to justify the device of dual voice-overs, which had seemed a risky proposition at the start. As brilliant as Hornby's dialogue is, you're letting down the side if you can't capture the tone and content of his internal narrative, and the best way we could figure it was to risk the taboo of telling as well as showing. The inspiration for this came from an unlikely source, Martin Scorsese's *Casino*, which had such a clever and pliant use of voice-over to intensify and underscore the action.

While we were working on the script, we kept playing Badly Drawn Boy's album *Hour of the Bewilderbeast* to get us in the right mood. And we started fantasizing about having him be the musical voice of the film (a decision which made us seem cool to Nick Hornby). It took a leap of faith on the part of Working Title and Universal to put the score in the hands of Badly Drawn Boy, and we're grateful for it. Badly Drawn Boy a.k.a. Damon Gough or, as we came to call him, The Badly showed a work ethic that belied his somewhat shaggy appearance and we were practically swamped with beautiful music for the movie. It was a great advantage that he was on board quite early, and could come to the set, see dailies, and be shown cut footage during the shooting of the movie, so that we could even time certain sequences to his music instead of the other way 'round. Since we had excised the thematic and plot elements surrounding Kurt Cobain's suicide from book to film, it was incredibly important to us to have such a strong thread running throughout.

The biggest change from book to script that readers of *About a Boy* will notice is the ending or, as the convention of film would have it, the "Third Act." It would be redundant to say that the end of the film is less novelistic than the book. We were keen to keep the focus of the end of the picture on our two main characters and to locate the final sequences in a setting we had already established, furthermore one full of dread not only for Marcus but, we think, for Will as well. The use of "Killing Me Softly," a beautiful and vulnerable song we remembered well from childhood, was just a playing out of a theme suggested earlier in Hornby's book by Will's horror at the lack of social armor Fiona and Marcus sported. We saw it as a fit resting point for Will and Marcus; after all, it's not really an ending, as Hornby implies at the end of his book. And if it is an ending, we were hoping not for a Hollywood Ending or even a Happy Ending but, to coin a phrase, an Okay Ending, which is a good place for these characters to find after all they've been through.

ABOUT A BOY

Screenplay
by
Peter Hedges
and
Chris Weitz & Paul Weitz

Based on the book
by
Nick Hornby

OVER A BLACK SCREEN

We hear the voice of a GAMESHOW ANNOUNCER reading off a
question.

                    GAMESHOW ANNOUNCER
              The Question is -- who wrote the
              phrase, "No man is an island." Was
              it -- a)John Donne, b)John F.
              Kennedy, or c) John Bon Jovi.

INT. WILL'S FLAT - DAY

We open on a fishtank; or rather, THROUGH a fishtank, in
which trendy, expensive tropical fish and miniature sharks
swim (if we have a weird experience of scale -- i.e. that the
sharks are really normal size sharks, that's okay, as a
matter of fact, it's good.

                    WILL (V.O.)
              Well that's an easy one.
              Definitely the most crap Bon Jovi
              lyric ever.

Through the fishtank, we see a trendy flat -- the home of a
bachelor of independent means. We see WILL, 38, unattached,
as he moves through it...

                    WILL (V.O.) (CONT'D)
              The way I see it, every man is an
              island.

...Or rather, we see PIECES of him, not his face yet, as he
strolls through his place getting ready to go out.
Underneath the V.O., very quietly, we hear the patter of the
game show continuing.

                    WILL V.O.
              But the great thing is, there's
              never been a better time in history
              to be an island. Even fifty years
              ago, for instance, they didn't have
              daytime TV --

We see Will's hand loom into frame and turn off the TV.

                    WILL V.O. CONT'D
              Or videos, or CD's, or home
              espresso makers, or glossy
              magazines with questionnaires about
              how cool you were and pictorials of
              scantily - clad models from Brazil.

As Will talks, we follow him as he goes to fetch his coat, and pass by various indications of his lifestyle.

> WILL V.O. CONT'D (CONT'D)
> *The thing was, every man was an*
> *island, but you didn't have to be a*
> *crap island.*

> WILL V.O. CONT'D (CONT'D)
> *With the right supplies, and the*
> *right outlook, you could be a sun-*
> *drenched tropical resort, the kind*
> *caressed by warm breezes, the kind*
> *with a permissive, carefree*
> *atmosphere, the kind visited by*
> *cute Swedish tourists on holiday.*

Will picks up a piece of paper that reads, "Kristina -- 7865-9878 -- call me!", crumples it up, and throws it in the bin as he heads out. We finally see his face as he walks to the door...

> WILL CONT'D V.O
> *Sure, I was an island, but I was a*
> *pretty cool island. I was Maui.*

Will heads out the door.

3   EXT. WILL'S STREET - DAY   3

We see Will through the window of his car as he EXITS into the street (overexposed).

> WILL (V.O.)
> *All the same, I was forced to visit*
> *the mainland from time to time, and*
> *observe their strange and barbaric*
> *ways.*

INSERT of Will's hand flicking the switchblade-like keys of his car. Then Will's hand turning the key of his car -- the whine of the highly tuned engine blends into the sound of a BABY CRYING. Then the TYRES SCREECH as he pulls out.

4   INT. CHRISTINE'S APARTMENT - DAY   4

The BABY'S CRYING continues. CHRISTINE, an attractive woman in her mid-thirties, comes towards Will holding out a

SCREAMING BABY.

                    CHRISTINE
               (proud)
          Will...this is Imogen! You can
          hold her if you like.

                    WILL
          Ah. Yes. Thank you.

Christine thrusts baby Imogen into Will's hands. Will holds
her gingerly away from his Prada shirt.

                    WILL (CONT'D)
          She's...
               (thinks; what are you
                supposed to say)
          ...delightful?

                    CHRISTINE
          Isn't she?

                    WILL
          Yes. But I think she smells my
          fear. Perhaps you'd better...

Christine takes the baby back.

                    CHRISTINE
               (cocks her head)
          Imagine...she could have been
          yours, if you'd got your act
          together..

                    WILL
          Your place looks marvellous.

They glance around the apartment, which looks like a
hurricane hit it. Plastic toys all over the place. Videos
strewn about. The white throw on the couch has a brown smear
on it near where Will is sitting.

                    WILL (CONT'D)
          I hope that's chocolate.

The joke doesn't register on Christine. JOHN, Christine's
husband, comes into the room, carrying Barney, a hyperactive
two-year-old.

                    JOHN
          Say hello to Will, Barney!

                    WILL
               (V.O.)
          Oh God, it's the anti-Christ.
               (MORE)

                    WILL (cont'd)
               (out loud)
          Hello, Barney. How are you.

                    JOHN
          Barney's a right little devil
          today, and he's not too sure what
          to make of Imogen, but...he's
          lovely.

Barney is making a growling expression and glaring at Will
like a pit bull.

                    WILL
          Yeeesss. So...Christine, what have
          you been up to?

                    CHRISTINE
               (beat)
          Well...I just had a baby, so that's
          pretty much what I've been up to.

                    WILL
          Of course.

                    JOHN
          What about you, Will? How are you?
          Any desire for a family of your
          own, yet?

                    WILL (O.S.)
          *I'd rather eat one of Barney's
          dirty nappies.*
               (aloud)
          Not yet. I'm okay as I am.

                    CHRISTINE
          Oh, please, Will.

                    WILL
          Please Will? Please Will what?

                    CHRISTINE
          Take a look at yourself. You're
          38, you've never had a job, or a
          relationship that lasted more than
          two months, except for me, and I
          chucked you because you were
          hopeless.

                    WILL
          Actually, didn't I chuck you?

>   CHRISTINE
>   It was mutual! The point is, I
>   wouldn't exactly say you're okay.
>   As a matter of fact, you're a
>   disaster. I mean what's the point
>   of your life?

Will looks shocked. It takes a moment for him to respond.

>   WILL
>   (covering)
>   ...Point of my life...very good
>   question...do you want that in five
>   words or less?

>   JOHN
>   She doesn't really mean it, Will.
>   It's the hormones. We just want
>   you to be as happy as we are.

John is trying to pry Barney's little hands off his throat.

>   WILL (V.O.)
>   *God, it's like a cult. They're
>   trying to recruit me.*

>   JOHN
>   Will, we wanted you to come over
>   today, so we could ask you...

>   CHRISTINE
>   ...How would you like to be
>   Imogen's Godfather?

Christine and John smile at Will expectantly.

>   WILL
>   Christine. John. I am truly,
>   truly...touched. But you must be
>   kidding. I couldn't possibly think
>   of a worse godfather for Imogen.
>   I'd drop her on her head at the
>   christening, then I'd forget about
>   her birthdays until her eighteenth,
>   when I'd take her out, get her
>   drunk and try to shag her.
>   Seriously. Very bad choice.

John and Christine look a little horrified.

>   CHRISTINE
>   I just...I always thought you had
>   hidden depths, Will.

                              WILL
                    But I don't. I really am this
                    shallow.

Will smiles. We stay on the smile a beat too long as we hear
a metallic TICKING sound.

5   INT. MARCUS'S BEDROOM - NIGHT   5

        -- And we realize that the TICKING is coming from an old-
        style alarm clock, the kind a kid has in his bedroom. A
        little green glow-in-the dark luminescence comes off the
        hands. It's five A.M. Marcus, 12 years old, lies awake in
        bed, looking apprehensive. A hamster in a cage RUNS on a
        tiny wheel.

6   INT. FIONA'S FLAT - NIGHT   6

        Marcus sits in various spots in the flat as the sun comes up.

7   INT. MARCUS BEDROOM - MORNING   7

        Marcus lies in bed, fully dressed. Finally...BRRIIIINNNGGG.
        The alarm clock rings.

8   EXT. FIONA'S HOUSE - MORNING   8

        FIONA, 34, and her son MARCUS, 12, exit their flat and walk
        along at a brisk pace. (NOTE: Fiona's window has
        placards/stickers from Greenpeace, Labour, and SPAT in it)

                              MARCUS
                         (pause)
                    Mum, did you always know I was
                    going to be a vegetarian?

                              FIONA
                         (laughs)
                    Of course I did. I didn't decide
                    on the spur of the moment just
                    because we'd run out of sausages.

        She tightens his woolly scarf.

                              MARCUS
                    Did you ask me? If I wanted to be
                    a vegetarian?

                              FIONA
                    You mean when you were born? No. I
                    do the cooking, and I don't want to
                    cook meat, so you have to eat what
                    I eat.

                    MARCUS
But you don't let me go to
McDonald's either.

                    FIONA
Is this premature teenage
rebellion? I can't stop you going
to McDonald's. I'd just be
disappointed if you did.

                    MARCUS (V.O.)
Mum was disappointed about a lot of
things. At least that's how it
seemed lately.
          (out loud)
So...did Roger and you split up
because he liked McDonald's?

                    FIONA
Of course not. Are you being
funny?

                    MARCUS (V.O.
It was weird. Mum had known me my
whole life, so she must have known
I was never funny. Not on purpose
anyway. It seemed   like a
sensible question.

9   INT. FIONA'S HOUSE - DINING ROOM - FLASHBACK, MORNING   9

We open tight on one of those odd trivia QUESTIONS that they
put on the back of cereal boxes as a fun-and-games thing for
kids, like, "When did Vasco De Gama cross the equator?" The
V.O. continues as we see Marcus intently staring at the
cereal box as we hear HUSHED MUTTERING in the background.

ROGER, forty or so, rumpled and unshaven, walks out of the
KITCHEN (we'll come to learn it's the kitchen of Marcus and
Fiona's house) into the dining room, and looking at Marcus.

                    MARCUS (V.O.)
Mum and Roger had a big row, then
they'd gone off into the kitchen to
talk quietly. Then Roger came out.

Roger stands in front of Marcus, looking at him. He HOLDS
OUT HIS HAND TO SHAKE. Marcus looks at him, takes his hand,
and shakes it.

Roger heads out, stops, look back at Marcus, shakes his head,
and leaves.

10   EXT. LONDON STREET - DAY   10

We pick up Fiona and Marcus's walk, and their conversation.

>   MARCUS
>   Then why did you split up with
>   Roger? Did he have another
>   girlfriend?

>   FIONA
>   I don't think so.

>   MARCUS
>   Do you have another boyfriend?

>   FIONA
>   (laughs)
>   Don't you think you would know? Who
>   would I be seeing, the milk man?

>   MARCUS
>   (seriously)
>   No. He's too young.

>   FIONA
>   No, Marcus. I haven't got another
>   boyfriend. That's not how it
>   works. Not when you're a thirty-
>   four-year old working mother in a
>   youth-obsessed, anorexic, soulless
>   culture.

Marcus looks up.

>   MARCUS
>   I won't go to McDonald's, Mum.
>   Don't worry.

Will's CAR drives past them. They walk on.

11   EXT. SCHOOL - DAY   11

Marcus and Fiona come to a stop outside Marcus's new school.
Big metal fences surround a truly grim Victorian pile. The
rest of the school is arriving for the morning. Some COOL-
LOOKING KIDS are taking their ease outside. Marcus looks up
at the other kids, scared.

>   FIONA
>   Well...here we are.

                              MARCUS
                        (looking around)
                  You know, you don't have to walk me
                  to school anymore, Mum. I know the
                  way now.

                              FIONA
                  What if I like walking you to
                  school?

She tightens his scarf again.

                              FIONA (CONT'D)
                        (looks him in the eye)
                  Right. Who are you?

                              MARCUS
                  I'm me.

                              FIONA
                  What are you not?

                              MARCUS
                  A sheep.

                              FIONA
                  Right. And what does a sheep go?

                              MARCUS AND FIONA
                        (together)
                  BAAA.

Fiona smiles, starts straightening Marcus's tie. We see that
the COOL KIDS are observing him.

                              MARCUS
                  Then I realized she was about to
                  kiss me goodbye.

We see Marcus straightening, looking over at the COOL KIDS.

                              MARCUS (V.O.) (CONT'D)
                  I decided to let her. Maybe it
                  would make her feel better.

Fiona leans over and kisses Marcus goodbye. Marcus closes
his eyes and lets it happen, taking pains not to wriggle
away. But that's not enough for Fiona...she HUGS HIM
TIGHTLY, as though he were going away for a year.

Marcus walks towards school, through some kids.

                         FIONA
                    (calls out)
               Marcus --
                    (from the bottom of her
                    soul)
               I love you.

The COOL KIDS see everything...

                         MARCUS
                    (quietly)
               I love you too...

Fiona heads off and Marcus turns and heads into school, past
a few COOL KIDS, who SNIGGER as he passes and call after him
in fake MUM VOICES --"I love love love you!", "Take good
care, sweety!", "Don't wet your pants!", etc. Marcus
pretends to ignore them, but we can see the FEAR register on
his face as he goes inside, past ELLIE, a punky girl with her
own little clique, who pays him no attention.

12   EXT. TRENDY RESTAURANT - NIGHT   12

Will walks down the street towards a trendy restaurant.

                         WILL (V.O.)
               While I couldn't accept Christine
               and John's disturbing offer to
               become their child's godfather, I
               did allow them to set me up with
               Angie, a rather beautiful co-worker
               of Christine's. But cruelly,
               nastily, Christine neglected to
               tell me one thing.

13   INT. TRENDY RESTAURANT - NIGHT   13

Will sits across the table from Angie, a beautiful thirty-
five year old.

                         ANGIE
               There's something you don't know
               about me.

                         WILL
                    (suggestively)
               Something exciting?

                         ANGIE
               Well, I think so, yes.
                    (pause)
               I have a three year old boy.

                         WILL
                    (V.O.)
               I wanted to throw the napkin on the
               floor, push over the table and run.
                    (casually)
               No problem. I love children.

Amgie smiles, surprised.

                         WILL (CONT'D)
               I enjoy messing about with them.
               Doing kid things. I would have
               been disappointed if you didn't
               have a child.

                         ANGIE
               Why do you say that?

                         WILL
                    (V.O)
               I don't know, mainly because it
               sounded smooth and winning.
                    (aloud)
               Because I love kids, they're
               so...lovely.
                    (V.O)
               What the hell are you saying, you
               pillock? She can't be buying this
               rubbish.

14   EXT. ZOO - DAY   14

Angie looks on happily --

                         WILL (V.O.)
               But she did buy my rubbish. For
               the next few weeks I was Will the
               Good Guy. Angie's kid took to me
               right away.

We can hear the SCREAMING laughter of a child -- and we pan
to reveal --

WILL, HOLDING A THREE YEAR OLD UPSIDE DOWN BY HIS ANKLES.

                         WILL (V.O.) (CONT'D)
               Mostly because on our first meeting
               I took him to the zoo and held him
               upside-down by his ankles. I wish
               relationships with proper human
               beings were that easy.

                         ANGIE
                    (laughing)
              Will, you are brilliant.

                         WILL (V.O.)
              And I came to realize that with
              single mums...

Angie walks out of frame and into --

15   INT. ANGIE'S LIVING ROOM - NIGHT   15

Angie's living room, which is in dark and sensual mode. Angie
refreshes Will's glass of Barolo.

                         WILL (V.O.)
              Particularly the ones who'd been
              messed around and eventually
              abandoned by the father of their
              children, you became, by
              comparison, well -- wonderful.

                         ANGIE
              Will, you're a wonderful person.

                         WILL
              Oh. Well...thank you.

Angie LUNGES for him, knocking the glass of wine out of his
hands as she kisses him passionately...

                         WILL (V.O.) (CONT'D)
              And the thing was, I didn't just
              seem like a better person, I seemed
              like a better lover. Not because
              of my extraordinary technique, but
              because her only other male company
              was a three year old.

16   INT. OUTSIDE ANGIE'S BEDROOM - NIGHT   16

OVER A SHOT OF ANGIE'S BEDROOM DOOR we HEAR:

                         ANGIE
              Will, you're -- <u>Will</u> -- **Will** --
              WILL!

                         WILL
                    (freaked, trying to shush
                     her)
              Angie -- the -- kid -- will --
              hear!

17   INT. INSIDE ANGIE'S BEDROOM - TIGHT ON CORNER OF BED   17

We see a smiley PLUSH TOY bouncing up and down on the edge of Angie's bed.

18   EXT. PARK - DAY   18

>   WILL (V.O.)
>   *But it was hard work to be*
>   *wonderful all the time.*

Will and Angie sit on a park bench with Angie's kid, eating fast-food burgers and chips. Will realizes he's out of chips. While Angie's not looking, Will spies come chips belonging to the kid, and steals them.

19   EXT. MOVIE THEATER - NIGHT   19

Will waits outside the Rialto, a trendy arthouse theater. Will is looking at his watch, annoyed, when Angie shows up. Will forces a smile and kisses her.

>   WILL (V.O.)
>   *...And eventually I began to wonder*
>   *whether Angie was exactly what I*
>   *was looking for. For instance, one*
>   *night she was late for the new IMAX*
>   *movie because the baby-sitter*
>   *hadn't turned up. That pissed me*
>   *off. And there were deeper*
>   *problems than that.*

20   INT. ANGIE'S LIVING ROOM NIGHT   20

Will and Angie sit on Angie's couch watching TV. (We don't see it; it's close to camera, so we can make out Will's pained expression). We hear bad melodramatic TV MUSIC.

>   WILL (V.O.)
>   *She didn't have a VCR or a*
>   *satellite or cable, so we were*
>   *always stuck watching some crap*
>   *made-for-TV movie about a kid with*
>   *a disease.*

>   DOCTOR (O.S.)
>   (on TV)
>   I'm afraid there's nothing we can
>   do.

>   WOMAN'S VOICE
>   (hysterical)
>   Oh God...Oh please, please no...

21   INT. TRENDY RESTAURANT - DAY   21

Will and Angie are eating. Will is thinking, trying to find
the right time to broach something unpleasant.

                    WILL (V.O.)
          I had to end it. But having been
          Will the Good Guy, I didn't relish
          going back to my usual role of Will
          the unreliable, emotionally stunted
          heartbreaker.

MATCH CUT FLASHBACK to various women sitting in seat where
Angie is sitting.

                    OLD GIRLFRIEND #1
               (cold)
          I'm sorry, <u>you're</u> breaking up with
          <u>me?</u> You

                    OLD GIRLFRIEND #2
               (crying)
          -- self-centered bastard, I --

                    OLD GIRLFRIEND #3
               (angry)
          -- can't believe I wasted my time
          on you, you --

                    OLD GIRLFRIEND #4
               (amazed)
          -- useless superficial loser!

Will's look seems to be in response to the attacks.

                    ANGIE
          Will...

We are back to the present: Will and Angie.

                    WILL (V.O.)
          And then, something magical
          happened.

                    ANGIE
          Will, I'm sorry, but I'm not sure
          this is working out. It's not you.
          You've been great. It's me. Well,
          my situation, anyway. With Louis,
          and his Dad...I'm not ready to
          launch into a relationship with
          anybody new yet.

                              WILL
                         (amazed at his luck)
                    ...I think I understand...

Will reaches out and takes her hand, gives her an
understanding look. Angie starts tearing up.

                              ANGIE
                    You're a wonderful, wonderful,
                    wonderful man, Will...I'm so
                    sorry...

                              WILL (V.O.)
                    *I'd never watched a woman cry
                    without feeling responsible before.
                    I could bestow forgiveness. It
                    felt amazing.*
                         (out loud)
                    You don't have to be sorry for
                    anything. Really.

Angie lowers her head, crying. Will discreetly gives a
nearby waiter the waving-hand-holding-a-pen signal to get the
check.

22   INT. WILL'S FLAT - SITTING ROOM - DAY   22

Will sits there, savoring the breakup, listening to cool
music, drinking foreign beer, smiling. Then, he has an idea,
goes into the kitchen, comes back with the Yellow Pages,
looks under S...

                              WILL (V.O.)
                    *The end of Angie...the beginning of
                    something else. It seems crazy
                    now, but I thought I was onto a
                    great idea. A revelation, in fact:
                    single mothers. Passionate sex, a
                    lot of ego massage, and a guilt-
                    free parting -- what more could a
                    man want? And there must be
                    thousands of them, just waiting for
                    a nice guy to sleep with and break
                    up with. Available, bright,
                    gorgeous single mothers...*

23   INT. FIONA'S FLAT - KITCHEN - DAY   23

Fiona is CRYING HER EYES OUT. She looks like hell. SNOT
dribbles from her nose. She barely has the energy to wipe it
away.

> MARCUS (V.O.)
> *I think Mum was depressed.*

A mournful Joni Mitchell song about how you don't need a piece of paper from the City Hall to stay together is playing. We see Marcus looking at her his mouth open.

> MARCUS (V.O.) (CONT'D)
> *The crying had started again, and*
> *it scared me. Because now it was*
> *in the mornings. Before breakfast.*
> *She'd never done that before.*
> (aloud)
> May I have some cocoa puffs?

> FIONA
> (crying)
> ...No...it's not Sunday...

> MARCUS (V.O.)
> *She was still Mum, of course.*

Fiona takes down a box of ANCIENT GRAINS cereal -- No Preservatives, No Added Sugar -- from the cupboard. She reaches up for a bowl, which is blocked by some hastily-stacked plates. This sends her into a fresh wave of tears.

> MARCUS (V.O.) (CONT'D)
> *I couldn't figure it out. Nobody*
> *was dead. She had a job as a music*
> *therapist, which is a kind of*
> *teacher for sick kids, so there was*
> *enough money for food and*
> *everything. And she was the one*
> *who got rid of Roger.*
> (aloud)
> Should I fix my own breakfast?

> FIONA
> No. I've got it.

Fiona pours milk over the cereal. The milk hits the cereal and splashes out onto the counter. This minor defeat brings another wave of anguish.

> FIONA (CONT'D)
> (crying)
> Oh God...

She composes herself, comes back into the dining room with the cereal and sits next to Marcus. She fixes his shirt collar.

                    FIONA (CONT'D)
       ...So...are you...looking forward
       to school today?...

Fiona breaks into fresh tears before Marcus can answer.

24   INT. SCHOOLROOM - DAY   24

Marcus sits in class, looking at a math textbook as the
teacher does a problem at the chalkboard.

We can see that Marcus's mind is wandering. As he begins to
think of his Mum, he starts HUMMING the Joni Mitchell song
she was playing that morning.

We see OTHER KIDS notice that Marcus is humming...jabbing
others in the ribs. Soon everybody is noticing it...

But Marcus is oblivious. His humming gets louder, past the
point of just humming-to-yourself humming...

And finally the TEACHER notices. Looks up. Marcus starts to
sing.

                    MARCUS
        (sings)
       We don't neeeeed no piece of paper
       from city hall --

He opens his eyes, sees that everyone is looking at him.
Everyone bursts out LAUGHING at Marcus, including the
teacher.

25   EXT. SCHOOLYARD - DAY   25

Marcus walks along the fence of the school's concrete
exercise yard. Word has clearly gotten around, and
everywhere he goes, kids are SINGING at him, throwing in
nonsense words. Marcus keeps walking, trying to ignore them,
and then stops in front of NICKY and MARK, two equally geeky-
looking losers, who are the closest thing Marcus has to
friends at this point.

                    MARCUS
       Hi, Nicky, Hi Mark. Are you going
       to Computer Club later?

A FOOTBALL slams into the fence near them. We follow the
ball's return path to where --

Some older kids, led by the thuggish LEE HARTLEY, come up
behind Marcus.

                              LEE HARTLEY
                    Oi, Madonna! Give us a song!

Another of the tough kids kicks the ball at them again;
Marcus, Nicky and Mark dodge it.

                              ANOTHER OLDER KID
                    It's not just Madonna. There's
                    three of them

                              LEE HARTLEY
                    Oh, yeah. I forgot. Oi. Spice
                    Girls! Do you lot know what a blow
                    job is?

WHAM! The soccer ball flies at them, hits Nicky and bounces
off.

                              LEE HARTLEY (CONT'D)
                    Shit. You made me lose my
                    football.

The cool kids head off after the ball. The three losers
stand there for a bit. Then Mark looks over at Nicky. They
share a look.

                              MARK
                    Marcus, we don't want you hanging
                    around with us anymore.

                              MARCUS
                    ...Why not?

                              MARK
                    Because of them.

                              MARCUS
                    They've got nothing to do with me.

                              MARK
                    Yes they do. We never had trouble
                    with anyone before we knew you, and
                    now we get this every day.
                    Everyone thinks you're weird.

                              MARCUS
                         (thinks)
                    Oh. Okay.

Marcus walks off, looking blank. The football flies towards
his head and we --

FREEZE FRAME, the ball inches from his head.

                    MARCUS (CONT'D)
          So there you have it. I was having
          a shit time at home and a shit time
          at school.

Time restarts and BOOM -- the ball hits him.

26   INT. TRENDY SUPERMARKET - DAY   26

Will wheels a cart down the aisle of the trendy supermarket
he frequents.

                    WILL
               (V.O., under this
               repeated)
          It was all very well deciding that
          single mums were the future...

Will sees a beautiful woman with a little girl in tow.
Smiles, starts edging towards her. The woman's husband joins
her with carrying a packet of pasta. Will edges away,
disappointed.

                    WILL (V.O.) (CONT'D)
          ...but the frustrating truth was
          that I didn't have any of their
          numbers. Where did they hang out?

27   EXT. NEWS KIOSK - DAY   27

Will, buying magazines, sees a posterboard containing notices
for flats, dog groomers, babysitters...and an advertisement
for a local self-help group: a hand-written sign that says:
"SPAT -- SINGLE PARENTS, ALONE TOGETHER". Meetings every
Friday at 2.00 PM, All-Purpose Room, Clerkenwell Town Hall."

28   EXT. TOWN HALL - DAY   28

Will walks up to the local town hall. Takes a deep breath,
sees a xerox copy of the sign we saw at the news kiosk.

                    WILL
               (aloud, to himself)
          I'm a single father. I have a two
          year old boy. I'm a single father.
          I have a two year old boy.
               (VO)
          SPAT. A veritable goldmine of
          single mums. I could see the
          beautiful creatures now, getting
          roaring drunk, forgetting their
          troubles, ready to rock and roll...

29   OMIT   29

30   INT. FUNCTION ROOM - DAY   30

We are in the middle of the circle of chairs, panning around
as the various single Mums exchange stories of woe. They are
not beautiful, and they are not drunk. One of them is
wearing a Lorena Bobbitt t-shirt.

                    MOIRA
          That was when I was seven months
          pregnant. By the time I had the
          baby, he was in Majorca with
          another woman. Not even the one
          that he cheated on me with the
          first time.

                    FRANCES
               (nods)
          With me, it was a week before the
          birth. He said I'd got too fat.

                    CAROLINE
          Mine was shagging his secretary.
          It's such a bloody cliche.

                    WILL (V.O.)
          I tell you one thing. Men are
          bastards. After about ten minutes,
          I wanted to cut my own penis off
          with a kitchen knife.

The circle has come around to Will. He's clearly expected to
speak.

                    WILL (CONT'D)
          Ah. Yes. Me. Well. I have a two
          year old, Ned. Blue eyes. Sandy
          hair. About...Two foot three, or
          so.
               (beat, lamely)
          Likes to be held upside down...

These details don't seem to be gripping his audience. So...

                    WILL (CONT'D)
               (brightly)
          His mother left.

The women seemed surprised.

                    FRANCES
          Really?

                    WILL
          Really. It was...a great shock.
          We were so happy...Sandra's
          neurology practice was finally up
          and running...and then one day, her
          bags are packed, and my best friend
          is waiting outside in his Ferrari.
          The new Modena, you know, the
          supercharged one.
               (off their looks)
          ...are there any other men in SPAT,
          at all?

We see that all the others are women, a wide assortment, but
no-one fitting Will's bill. Except one. Suzie.

                    SUZIE
          Just one, Jeremy. He's on holiday.

                    WILL
               (relieved)
          So his wife left too.

                    SUZIE
               (shakes her head)
          Jeremy's wife was killed in a car
          crash.

                    WILL
          Oh.
               (pause)
          So I'm on my own.

Some sympathetic moans from the women. MOIRA, the one
wearing the Lorena Bobbitt t-shirt, chips in.

                    MOIRA
               (cheerily)
          You got dumped, then?

                    WILL
               (brightly)
          Yes!
               (then, wistfully)
          Yes.

                    SUZIE
          And does your ex see Ned?

                    WILL
          Sometimes. Not that she's really
          bothered.

REACTIONS from the women. Will is pleased.

                    SUZIE
         How does he cope with that?

                    WILL
              (getting into it)
         Oh, he's a good little boy. Very
         brave.
              (pause, off their looks)
         They have amazing resources, don't
         they?   Just yesterday, I
         was...thinking about my ex, and
         he...he crawled right up to me, put
         his pudgy little arms around my
         neck, and said...Dad...it's okay,
         Dad.

Will is actually blinking a tear from his eye.

                    SUZIE
         That's incredible for a two year
         old.

                    WILL
         Is it? Well, he's...very
         special...
         Sometimes I feel like it's...him
         who's taking care of me, teaching
         me the lessons of life...
              (V.O., as Will tears up a
               little)
         What a performance. I was even
         fooling myself. And by the end of
         the evening, I had a date lined up.

CUT TO LATER

The SPATS hold hands in a circle, CHANTING:

                    SPATS
         SINGLE PARENTS ALONE TOGETHER.
         SINGLE PARENTS ALONE TOGETHER.
         SINGLE PARENTS ALONE TOGETHER. ALL
         FOR ONE AND ONE FOR ALL!

Will looks over at Suzie, who's holding hands with him. They
share a smile.

CUT TO

The group does trust exercises, falling into each others
arms. Will arranges himself so Suzie falls into Will's.

CUT TO

The group has split into twos, doing ROLE PLAYING
reenactments, emoting at each other. Suzie emotes at Will.
Will, enjoying it, emotes at Suzie.

31   EXT. MOTHERCARE - DAY   31

                        WILL (V.O.)
                  *The problem was, I also had an
                  imaginary two-year-old son.*

A gigantic chain baby-care store. Will's car PEELS into the
parking lot.

32   INT. MOTHERCARE - DAY   32

Will walks along the aisles, checking out various baby
paraphernalia.

CUT TO

Will is fascinatedly inspecting a BREAST MILK PUMP.
Tentatively puts the cup to his chest.

CUT TO

Will is playing with a musical toy that plays "Twinkle
Twinkle Little Star" in doggy woofs, duck quacks, or sheep
baaas, depending on which button you push. He's enjoying it.

CUT TO

Will inspecting some cans of baby food. Opens one and tries
it. Not bad.

CUT TO

The car seat area. Will ambles up to the shop assistant.

                        WILL
                  I'm looking for a car seat.

                        ASSISTANT
                  What type are you looking for?

                        WILL
                  Dunno. Anything. The cheapest.
                        (laughs)
                  What do most people get?

                    ASSISTANT
          Well, not the cheapest. Parents
          are usually worried about safety.

                    WILL
          Ah. Yes. Not much point in saving
          a few quid if he ends up through
          the windscreen, is there?

                    ASSISTANT
               (beat)
          Yeah.

                    WILL
          That's a cool one!

                    ASSISTANT
          Of course even if you get a nice
          one, the kids mess them all up
          anyway with their sweets and all
          that.

Will nods.

33   EXT. MOTHERCARE - DAY   33

Will has a candy bar and a packet of crisps/chips. He pours
BABY FOOD, CANDY AND CRISPS onto the baby seat, and GRINDS
THEM IN WITH HIS SHOES. A passing mother looks at him like
he's crazy.

CUT TO

Will tries to jam the car-seat into the tiny back seat of his
sportscar.

34   OMIT   34

35   EXT. SUZIE'S HOUSE - DAY   35

Will's car drives down the street, pulls up.

                    WILL (V.O.)
          *The date was a SPAT picnic in
          Battersea Park with everyone
          bringing their kids. Sadly Ned
          couldn't be there. His mum had
          called round and picked him up at
          the last second.*

CUT TO

Will is standing with Suzie and her daughter Megan on the
street.

> SUZIE
> Oh, what a shame. Well this is
> Megan.

> WILL
> Great.

> SUZIE
> (leans closer)
> And a friend of mine from SPAT's
> not feeling so great, so I told her
> I'd take her kid too -- hope that's
> okay.

> WILL
> (beat)
> The more the merrier.

> SUZIE
> (calls back to house)
> Come on, slowcoach.

Marcus trudges down the street, looking annoyed.

> MARCUS (V.O.)
> *I hated that SPAT lot. I mean,*
> *Mum's friend Suzie was fine, but*
> *now there was also this Wally who*
> *wanted to get off with her...*

> WILL
> Okay. Pile in, everyone. Whoa,
> look what a mess Ned made of the
> car seat. Shame he can't come.

Marcus notices the dirty car seat, and the spotlessly clean
interior of the rest of the car.

36   EXT. PARK - DAY   36

The picnic. Marcus strolls along besides Suzie.

> SUZIE
> What a bitch. Taking Ned off like
> that at the last moment. This is a
> nasty business, Will. You'll have
> to toughen up. You're too nice.

                    WILL
            (savouring "too nice")
      I know, you're right, she's...
            (thinks)
      A cow.

                    MARCUS
      Moooo.

Will looks at Marcus, who looks back blankly.

                    WILL (V.O.)
      I was beginning to wonder if we
      were going to be stuck with this
      weird kid all day.

                    SUZIE
      So...what do you do, Will?

                    WILL
      Me? Well...

Will looks a bit sheepish.

                    WILL (V.O.) (CONT'D)
      There were already too many lies to
      keep track of. So I told the
      truth.
            (real world)
      Nothing.

                    SUZIE
      Well what did you do before?

                    WILL
      Before I did nothing?

                    SUZIE
      Yes.

                    WILL
      I did nothing.

                    SUZIE
      You've never worked?

                    WILL
      I've done the odd day here and
      there, but...

                    SUZIE
      Oh, that's...

Will and Suzie walk along a bit, uncomfortable.

                    WILL
               (reluctantly)
          My dad wrote a song. In nineteen
          fifty-eight. It's a famous song,
          and I live off the royalties.

                    MARCUS
          You know Michael Jackson? He makes
          one million pounds a minute. Sixty
          million pounds an hour.

                    WILL
          Well, I don't make a million pounds
          a minute. Nothing like.

                    MARCUS
          How much then?

                    SUZIE
          Marcus. So what's this song? If
          you can live off it, we must have
          heard of it.

                    WILL
               (apprehensive)
          Umm...Santa's Super Sleigh.

                    SUZIE & MARCUS
               (singing, together)
          So just leave out the mince pies,
          and a glass of sherry, and Santa
          will visit you, and leave you
          feeling merry, Oh, ho ho ho, hey
          hey hey, it's Santa's super sleigh,
          Santa's super sleigh...

Will looks ashen.

                    SUZIE
          I expect people always do that,
          don't they?

                    WILL
          You two are the first, actually.

                    SUZIE
          Sorry.
               (pause)
          But I don't understand. How does
          that make money? Do carol singers
          have to pay you ten percent?

                    WILL
They should, but you can't always
catch the little bastards. No,
it's on every Christmas album ever
made. Elvis did it, you know. The
Muppets. And an American punk band
called Jesus Crotch.
        (changes the subject)
So, Marcus, who's your favorite
footballer?

                    MARCUS
I hate football.

                    WILL
Right. What a shame.

                    MARCUS
Why?

                    WILL
        (beat)
Who are your favorite singers then?

                    MARCUS
        (snorts)
Are you getting these questions out
of a book?

Suzie laughs. Will blushes, as Marcus walks a bit ahead.

                    WILL
        (quietly)
So, how often do you look after
Marcus?

                    SUZIE
        (quietly)
Oh, every once in a while. His mum
is a little...off colour sometimes.

                    MARCUS
        (he's heard them)
You call it off colour, I call it
nuts.

                    SUZIE
She's not nuts, Marcus. She just
needs a weekend taking it easy.
We'll have a nice picnic, and when
you get back tonight she'll be
rested up and ready to go.

                         WILL
               My God, what on earth is this?

     Will has removed a round, obviously heavy health loaf from
     Suzie's bag.

                         MARCUS
               My Mum's homemade bread.

                         WILL
                    (embarrassed)
               Looks delicious.

                         MARCUS
               It's not. It's healthy.

     Marcus picks it up and walks off.

37   EXT. NEARBY - POND - DAY   37

     Marcus, alone, is picking little pieces from the loaf,
     throwing them to some ducks in the pond, who hurry in to snap
     up the bread. We can hear their excited QUACKING.

     He pulls on the bread, but it's rock hard and a hassle to
     keep ripping off little shreds. He looks at the loaf, makes
     a decision, and throws the WHOLE THING to the ducks. We hear
     excited QUACKING as the great, stonehenge-evoking loaf
     hurtles through the air, and then we hear a THUD and the
     quacking suddenly STOPS. Marcus' face falls.

38   EXT. PARK - DAY   38

     Nearby, Will and Suzie are sitting down on a blanket. Some
     wine has been consumed. Something in the air. In the
     background, kids from the picnic play.

                         SUZIE
               You miss him, don't you?

                         WILL
               Who? Ah. Ned. Yes. I do.

                         SUZIE
               So...what does Ned look like?

                         WILL
               Well...he looks like me. He got
               the short end of the stick.

                         SUZIE
               I don't think it's the short end...

Will looks at Suzie. Suzie smiles at him. Will smiles back.

                    MARCUS (V.O.)
          Uh...Uh...

Marcus is there, hopping from foot to foot, as if he's about
to wet himself.

                    MARCUS (CONT'D)
              (upset)
          I think I've killed a duck.

39   EXT. NEARBY - POND - DAY   39

Will, Suzie, Marcus and Suzie's little girl Megan stand by
the side of the lake, looking at what is definitely a dead
duck, floating upside-down in the water, its webbed feet
sticking up in the air.

                    MARCUS
          I was just trying to feed it.

                    WILL
          What's that floating next to it? Is
          that your mum's bread?

We can see the loaf floating around near the duck. Marcus
nods unhappily.

                    WILL (CONT'D)
          Guess it wasn't so healthy after
          all.
              (beat)
          Did you have to throw the whole
          thing? That would have killed me.

A PARK-KEEPER appears, angry.

                    PARK-KEEPER
              (to Marcus)
          Are you the one who was throwing
          bloody great loaves of bread at the
          ducks?

Marcus looks up to Will, scared.

                    WILL
          Yes, he was. But I've stopped him
          now. Boys will be boys.

Marcus looks at Will, feeling betrayed.

                    PARK-KEEPER
          So he killed it. You know that's a
          criminal offense.

                    WILL
          What? Oh -- oh God no. Sorry. I
          see what you mean. No, he was
          throwing bread at the body. I
          think he was trying to sink it,
          because Megan here was getting
          upset.

The park-keeper looks at Megan, who is asleep.

                    PARK-KEEPER
          She doesn't look very upset.

                    WILL
          No. Cried herself to sleep, poor
          thing.

There's a silence. The park-keeper appears to be deciding
what to do.

                    WILL (CONT'D)
          Marcus wouldn't kill a duck. Would
          you, Marcus?

                    MARCUS
          No, I love ducks. They're my
          second favorite animal. After
          dolphins.
               (beat)
          Dolphins can kill sharks. With
          their noses.

The park-keeper, nonplussed, shakes his head.

                    PARK-KEEPER
               (annoyed)
          I'll have to wade in and get it.

And he heads off.

                    WILL
               (calls after him)
          I hope there's not some sort of
          epidemic.
               (to Marcus)
          I think we beat the rap, Marcus.

As soon as Will turns his back, Marcus <u>smiles</u>.

Then, over Will's shoulder, he sees FIONA. Standing on the
other side of the pond. She's smiling and waving at him.

                    MARCUS
                (to himself)
            Mum.

Marcus turns to Suzie.

                    MARCUS (CONT'D)
            Suzie, look, it's --

Marcus turns round again, but Fiona isn't there anymore.
Marcus looks confused.

40   EXT. FIONA'S FLAT - LATE AFTERNOON   40

Will pulls up in his car, and Marcus and he get out. Suzie
gets out too, carrying Megan. They head to the front door.

                    MARCUS (V.O.)
            That day, the Dead Duck Day, was
            when it all began.

41   INT. FIONA'S FLAT - FRONT DOOR - LATE AFTERNOON   41

The door opens, Marcus holding the key, Suzie and Megan and
Will behind him.

                    MARCUS (V.O.)
            That bloke Will just followed us
            in, and I didn't tell him not to.

Things have a sudden dreamlike quality. The textures of the
entrance hall, the colors, seem a little off. They are
walking up the stairs to the upper flat, where Marcus and
Fiona live.

                    MARCUS (V.O.) (CONT'D)
            Afterwards, I realized that there
            was no way I could have been
            nervous just then, because just
            then I didn't know there was
            anything to be nervous about.

Marcus sticks the key in the door of his flat. Opens it.

                    MARCUS (V.O.) (CONT'D)
            But then I put the key in the lock,
            opened the door, and --

42   INT. FIONA'S FLAT - SITTING ROOM - LATE AFTERNOON.   42

ANGLE ON FIONA --

Where Fiona is lying, half on, half off, her head lolling off
the couch. She is a ghastly shade of white, and there is a
pool of vomit on the ground. There's a bottle of pills lying
next to the pool of vomit.

                    WILL
          Jesus!

For a moment, they all just stand there. Then, Suzie, runs
past Marcus, jostling him. She runs to Fiona, an starts
shaking her.

                    SUZIE
          Will, call an ambulance! Marcus,
          make some coffee! Now!

But for the moment, Will and Marcus are both just standing
there, looking blank, as Suzie starts SHAKING and HITTING
Fiona, and little Megan starts CRYING.

                    MARCUS
               (to Will)
          How do you make coffee?

Now Fiona is moaning, a horrible, low sound.

                    SUZIE
          Fiona! Wake up!

                    MARCUS
          Why's she so angry at Mum?

Will looks down at Marcus.

                    MARCUS (CONT'D)
          She's sick, isn't she?

                    SUZIE
          How could you do this! You have a
          son!

Then Marcus sees the empty pill bottle. Suddenly Will seems
to wake from his trance.

                    WILL
          Marcus, where's the phone?

                                        CUT TO:

43   EXT. THAMES EMBANKMENT - LATE AFTERNOON   43

From high above, we see Will's car driving along the
embankment at high speed following an ambulance (HELICOPTER).

                    WILL (V.O.)
          This was horrible, horrible...but
          driving fast behind the ambulance
          was pretty cool.

44   INT. WILL'S CAR - SAME   44

Will and Marcus sit in the front seat of Marcus's car. Will
is racing after the AMBULANCE, trying to keep up. His tongue
is out in concentration.

45   INT. HOSPITAL EMERGENCY ROOM - NIGHT   45

Suzie sits there in the waiting room, which is populated
mostly with drunks -- stumbles, fistfights, DUI accidents.
Will, unscratched in his modish clothes, is like a creature
from another planet here.

                    WILL (V.O.)
          I mean, granted, it wasn't quite up
          to the level of a good episode of
          E.R., but I couldn't help getting
          sucked in.
               (out loud, brightly)
          So what's happening?

                    SUZIE
               (a little taken aback by
                Will's enthusiasm)
          She's conscious. She was okay in
          the ambulance.
               (to Marcus)
          She was asking after you, Marcus.

                    MARCUS
          That's nice of her.

                    SUZIE
          This isn't anything to do with you,
          Marcus. You know that, don't you?
          I mean, you're not the reason
          she...You're not the reason she's
          here. Right Will?

                    WILL
               (unsure)
          Right. Right right right.

Suzie heads over to a vending machine. Will looks over, not
wanting to be left alone with Marcus.

                    WILL (CONT'D)
          I can get the...tea...
               (pause; turning to Marcus)
          Your Mum's going to be okay.

                    MARCUS
          Yeah, I suppose so, but that's not
          the point, is it?

                    WILL
          What do you mean?

                    MARCUS
          Work it out for yourself.

                    WILL
          Are you afraid she'll try again?

                    MARCUS
          Just shut up, all right?

Suzie comes back.

                    SUZIE
          Milk and two sugars, the way you
          like it, Marcus.

                    NURSE
               (walking over)
          Are you with Fiona Brewer?

                    SUZIE
          Yes. I'm her friend Suzie, and
          this is...Will.

                    NURSE
          She's recovering well, but we're
          keeping her overnight. I'll go and
          get a consent form for Ms. Brewer
          so the boy can stay overnight with
          you two.

The nurse's gaze includes both Suzie and Will.

                    WILL
          Right then.
               (to Suzie, a bit
                suggestively)
          Your place or mine?

Suzie gives Will a very annoyed look.

                    WILL (CONT'D)
          Sorry.

46   EXT. SUZIE'S HOUSE - NIGHT   46

Will's car pulls up to a nondescript bunch of row-houses --
Suzie's house. He gets out, opens the door for Suzie.

                    WILL (V.O.)
          All in all, this had been very
          interesting, but I wouldn't want to
          do it every night.
          The thing was...a person's life was
          like a TV show. I was the star of
          the Will show.

Will leans in to kiss Suzie goodbye; she emphatically gives
him "The Cheek". Suzie takes Megan out from the car seat.

                    WILL (CONT'D)
          And the Will show wasn't an
          ensemble drama. Guests came and
          went, but I was the regular. It
          came down to me, and me alone.

Will looks at Marcus, standing next to him. Gives him a
playful punch on the arm.

                    WILL (CONT'D)
          See you soon.

Marcus seems set into motion.

                    WILL (CONT'D)
          If Marcus' mum couldn't manage her
          own show, if her ratings were
          falling, well, that was her
          problem. All in all, the single
          mum plotline was a bit complicated
          for me.

Will gets into the car and pulls away, and we are --

47   INT. WILL'S CAR - NIGHT   47

As Will looks at himself in the vanity mirror. Turns on his
stereo.

48   EXT. WILL'S CAR - NIGHT   48

He drives off into the night.

                                        CUT TO:

49   INT. FIONA'S FLAT - KITCHEN - DAY   49

Marcus is tidying the apartment. He sets the table. He puts
flowers in a vase, and finds a letter in a blue envelope
sitting by the sink. He picks it up and reads, frowning.

Marcus sits down. Reads the letter.

As he sits there, thinking, the LIGHT CHANGES, showing in
this quick scene, the entire day passing...and the room goes
dark.

50   INT. FIONA'S HOUSE - DINING ROOM - DUSK   50

Marcus looks out the window.

51   EXT. FIONA'S HOUSE - DUSK   51

From out of the window, we see Marcus' POV of a cab pulling
up, and Suzie gets out. Suzie helps Fiona out of the cab.

52   INT. FIONA'S HOUSE - SITTING ROOM - DUSK   52

Suzie HUGS Fiona. Then she comes over to where Marcus is
sitting on the couch.

                        SUZIE
                  (whispers loudly)
            Your mum's going to be **all right**.

Suzie smiles at Marcus and leaves.

53   INT. FIONA'S FLAT - DINING ROOM - NIGHT   53

Fiona fills the kettle. Marcus sits at the kitchen table.

                        MARCUS
            I got the letter. Thanks.

                        FIONA
            The -- Oh my God, I'd forgotten.

                        MARCUS
            You forgot? You forgot a suicide
            letter?

                    FIONA
Well I didn't think I'd have to
remember it, did I?

                    FIONA (CONT'D)
          (laughs; then)
     Did you read the part where I said
I'd always love you, and I'm sorry?

                    MARCUS
It's hard for you to love me when
you're dead, isn't it?

                    FIONA
I understand why you're angry,
Marcus. I don't feel the same as I
did yesterday, if that's any help.

                    MARCUS
What, it's all just gone away, all
that?

                    FIONA
No, but...at the moment, I feel
better.

                    MARCUS
At the moment's no good to me. I
can see you're better at the
moment. You've just put the kettle
on. But what happens when you've
finished your tea? What happens
when I go back to school? I can't
be here to watch you all the time.

                    FIONA
No, I know. But we've got to look
after each other. The two of us.

Marcus nods.

                    MARCUS (V.O.)
*Suddenly I realized -- two people
isn't enough. You need backup. If
you're only two people, and someone
drops off the edge, then you're on
your own. Two isn't a large enough
number.*
          (aloud)
You need three at least.

                    FIONA
Three what?

                    MARCUS
          ...Nothing.
                (V.O.)
          But I'd had a great idea.
                (aloud)
          What's Suzie's number?

54   INT. WILL'S FLAT - KITCHEN - DAY   54

     Will makes espresso on his fancy espresso machine.

                    WILL (V.O.)
          The important thing in island
          living is to be your own activities
          director.

55   INT. WILL'S FLAT - BATHROOM - DAY   55

     Will takes a bath.

                    WILL V.O.)
          It helps to think of the day as
          units of time, each unit consisting
          of thirty minutes. Most activities
          take about a half hour. Taking a
          bath.

56   INT. WILL'S FLAT - SITTING ROOM - DAY   56

     Will does a crossword puzzle.

                    WILL (V.O.)
          Doing the crossword.   Watching TV.

     CUT TO Will watching TV.

                    WILL(V.O.) (CONT'D)
          Doing research on the net. One
          unit.

     CUT TO Will on his computer. We see him type in the web
     address "WWW.HTTP//supermodelswithseethroughtops.com"

57   INT. SNOOKER HALL - DAY   57

                    WILL(V.O.)
          Exercising. Three units.

     Will pots a ball.

58   OMIT   58

59   INT. HAIR SALON - DAY   59

                         WILL (V.O.)
                    Carefully trimming my perfectly
                    unkempt hair...two units, easy.
                    All in all I had a very full life.

Will is getting his HAIR SHAMPOOED in a salon when his MOBILE
PHONE RINGS. The salon assistant towels his hair as Will
answers the phone.

                         WILL (CONT'D)
                    Will here.

                         MARCUS (O.S.)
                    It's Marcus.

                         WILL
                    Pardon?

60   OMIT   60

61   INT. FIONA'S FLAT - SITTING ROOM - DAY   61

                         MARCUS
                    It's Marcus.

62   INT. HAIR SALON (INTERCUT)   62

                         WILL
                    ...Marcus? Oh, <u>Marcus</u>. How did
                    you get my number?

The hair stylist puts a BIB on Will, preparing to cut his
hair.

He smiles up at the hair stylist as if to say -- "I'm not
crazy, I'm just kidding around."

                         MARCUS (O.S.)
                    From Suzie. I thought you'd like
                    to take me out for the day on
                    Saturday.

                         WILL
                    Why did you think that, Marcus?

                         MARCUS (O.S.)
                    Suzie said we hit it off.

                         WILL
                    Did she.

                    MARCUS (O.S.)
          And you said "See you soon".

                    WILL
          I said what?

                    MARCUS (O.S.)
          "See you soon." The night you
          dropped us off you said "see you
          soon", remember?

                    WILL
          Well, this is...soon, alright.
          Look, Marcus, life's kind of hectic
          for me at the moment, so...

                    MARCUS
          Why? I thought you did nothing.

                    WILL
          Well, I'm taking care of Ned,
          aren't I? As a matter of fact
          we're on the way to preschool right
          now, and --

The stylist fires up a pair of clippers. Marcus overhears
the buzz.

                    MARCUS
          What's that?

                    WILL
          Lawnmower. Look, Marcus, this is
          just not going to work...
               (V.O.)
          -- *but then I thought, why not?*

The stylist is working on his hair.

                    WILL (V.O.) (CONT'D)
          Why shouldn't I take the poor
          little freak out for a meal? I
          could be Uncle Will. Cool Uncle
          Will, King of the Kids.
               (aloud)
          Okay, Marcus, you're on.

                    MARCUS (O.S.)
          I'll come if you take my mum, too.
          And she hasn't got any money, so
          either we'll have to go somewhere
          cheap or you'll have to treat us.

                    WILL
          Hey, Marcus, don't beat around the
          bush.

                    MARCUS (O.S.)
          Why should I? We're poor. You're
          rich. You pay. You can bring your
          little boy if you want. I don't
          mind.

                    WILL
          That's big of you Marcus.

                    MARCUS (O.S.)
          Fine. Come round at half-past
          twelve or something. You remember
          where we live? Flat 2, 31
          Craysfield Road, Islington, London,
          N1 2SF.

                    WILL
          England, the world, the Universe.

63   INT. FIONA'S FLAT - SITTING ROOM - DAY   63

                    MARCUS
               (blank)
          Yeah. And we'd like to go to
          Planet Hollywood.

64   INT. HAIR SALON - DAY   64

                    WILL
          Oh God, really?

                    MARCUS (O.S.)
          Yeah. I hear it's brilliant.

       Marcus hangs up.

65   EXT. CHURCH - DAY   65

       Will walks up to a church with some homeless people queued up
       by the side entrance.

                    WILL(V.O.)

          In fact, charitable impulses were a
          good way of using up units. Like
          that time I phoned and volunteered
          to help out at a soup kitchen.

       Will keeps on walking.

                              WILL (V.O.) (CONT'D)
                         And I almost made it.

66   INT. AMNESTY INTERNATIONAL - DAY   66

          We track along a line of right-on looking people on phones,
          making phone calls for an Amnesty pledge drive.

                              WILL(V.O.)
                         Or the time I volunteered at
                         Amnesty International.

                              RIGHT-ON PERSON #1
                              (fervent)
                         -- Did you know, for instance, that
                         in Burma you can be sentenced to
                         seven years in prison for telling
                         jokes? Next time you laugh, I want
                         you to think of Pa Pa Lay, the
                         Burmese stand up comedian!

                              RIGHT-ON PERSON #2
                         -- we're at a crucial stage in our
                         struggle for human rights in Burma,
                         which are being grossly abused by
                         the ruling military junta, and --

                              RIGHT-ON PERSON #3
                         -- we need your support more than
                         ever. Together we can make a
                         difference --

          Meanwhile, Will flirts over the phone with someone he's just
          cold-called.

                              WILL
                              (laughs)
                         You're kidding. So what does your
                         boyfriend think of that? Wait a
                         minute -- you're single? Talk
                         about human rights violations.

67   OMIT   67

68   EXT. PLANET HOLLYWOOD - DAY   68

          We go down a long queue of people queuing/waiting, speaking
          every language except English. The queue is reminiscent of
          the soup kitchen queue. Then there's Marcus, Will and Fiona.
          Will checks his watch.

> WILL
> Marcus, this is hopeless. Look at
> the queue.

> MARCUS
> (annoyed)
> That's probably because Bruce
> Willis is inside. Or Sylvester
> Stallone.

Both Will and Fiona laugh.

> FIONA
> Marcus, they won't be there, you
> know.

> MARCUS
> Yes they will. They're there all
> the time. Unless they're working.
> And even then they try to make
> films in London so they can come
> here for lunch.
> (thinks)
> I'm really hungry.
> (pause)
> Does that place you're talking
> about have good fries?

69   INT. TRENDY RESTAURANT - DAY   69

Will, Marcus and Fiona sit at lunch in the same trendy
restaurant we saw him in with Angie earlier. Marcus looks
around, annoyed, as he's handed a menu.

> WILL
> You said you liked chips, didn;t
> you? Well they have great chips
> here.

Marcus shrugs.

> WILL (CONT'D)
> (to Fiona)
> So...how are you...I mean...how are
> you feeling...

> FIONA
> My stomach's fine. I must still be
> a bit barmy, though. That kind of
> thing doesn't go away overnight,
> does it?

Will looks shocked, and buries his gaze in his menu.

> MARCUS (V.O.)
> *If Mum was going to get Will to*
> *marry her, she'd have to quit*
> *making jokes like that. At least*
> *she looked good -- I made her put*
> *on that nice hairy jumper, and*
> *those earrings she got sent from*
> *her friend that went to Zimbabwe.*

> WILL (V.O.)
> *The kid seemed to think this was*
> *some kind of date. The mum was*
> *clearly a barking lunatic. She was*
> *wearing some kind of wildebeest*
> *hide, and some elephant carvings*
> *that threatened to tear through her*
> *earlobes. She looked like the*
> *abominable snowman. This had*
> *better be a quick one. We were*
> *definitely not ordering starters.*

Meanwhile, a waiter has come up to take their order.

> MARCUS
> I'll start with the artichoke,
> please. Then I'll have a mushroom
> omelette and chips, please, and a
> coke.

> FIONA
> I'll have the vegetable platter.

> MARCUS
> We're vegetarians.

> WILL
> Ah.
> (to the waitress)
> Steak sandwich, please.

There's another silence.

> MARCUS
> Well don't just sit there.
> (off their looks)
> You heard me. Don't just sit
> there. Talk to each other.

> FIONA
> I'm not sure that's how
> conversation happens, Marcus.

                    WILL
               (laughs)
          No. He's right.

                    WILL (CONT'D)
          We probably have at least sixty
          years of conversational experience
          here. I'm sure we can manage
          something.

                    FIONA
          Okay, then.

                    WILL
          So.

                    FIONA
          After you.

They laugh. But they don't say anything. Marcus sighs.

                    MARCUS
          Will, why did your wife chuck you?

                    FIONA
          Marcus!

                    WILL
          No, that's okay. I feel okay
          talking about it now.
               (thinks)
          She went through this whole I-Want-
          To-Find-Out-Who-I-Am malarkey.

                    FIONA
          And did she find out who she was?

                    WILL
          Um...
               (V.O.)
          *She was a figment of my twisted
          imagination, that's who she was.*
               (out loud)
          Not really. I don't know if anyone
          really does, do they?

                    FIONA
               (smiles)
          We know who we are, don't we
          Marcus?

                    WILL (V.O.)
          That's right, you're a depressive
          hippy and her weirdo son.

                    MARCUS (V.O.)
          This was going really well. I
          wondered if we were going to move
          into Will's place, or move into
          someplace new.

70   INT. FIONA'S FLAT - SITTING ROOM - DAY   70

Fiona is playing the piano in her living room, singing with a
deadly sincere expression on her face.

                    FIONA
               (singing)
          I HEARD HE SANG A GOOD SOOONG...I
          HEARD HE HAD A STYLE... AND SO I
          CAME TO SEE HIM, TO LISTEN FOR A
          WHILE...AND THERE HE WAS, THIS
          YOUNG BOY, A STRANGER TO MY EYES...

We PULL BACK to reveal Will, who looks shocked. He turns and
stares at Marcus, who, far from joining Will in his chagrin,
begins SINGING ALONG.

                    FIONA AND MARCUS
               (singing)
          STRUMMING MY PAIN WITH HIS
          FINGERS, SINGING MY LIFE WITH HIS
          WORDS...KILLING ME SOFTLY WITH HIS
          SONG, KILLING ME SOFTLY...WITH HIS
          SONG...

                    WILL (V.O)
               (over singing)
          I knew, of course, that the song
          couldn't last forever, that I would
          soon be at home, tucked up in bed.
          I knew it, but I didn't feel it.
          The worst part was when they closed
          their eyes...
               (they do; we see Will
               cringe)
          I must have been crazy. All I'd
          wanted was a date with Suzie, and
          somehow I got mixed up with this
          poor kid.

                    MARCUS
          Come and sing the last verse with
          us, Will!

                    WILL
          Thanks, but I have to get going.

Marcus looks over at Will.

71   INT. SCHOOL - DAY   71

Marcus sits in class, looking at a maths book, thinking.

72   EXT. CLERKENWELL STREET - DAY   72

As Will walks, we see Marcus across the street, watching him.

                    WILL (V.O.)
          That was the problem with charity.
          You have to _mean_ things. You have
          to _mean_ things to help people.

                    WILL (V.O.) (CONT'D)
          Fiona _meant_ Killing Me Softly.
          Killing Me Softly _meant_ something
          to her. And look where she ended
          up.

73   INT . ENTRANCE TO TRENDY SUPERMARKET - DAY   73

Will goes into a trendy, upscale supermarket.

                    WILL (V.O.)
          Me, I didn't _mean_ anything. About
          anything, to anyone. And I knew
          that guaranteed me a long,
          depression-free life.

Marcus follows Will into the market.

74   INT. TRENDY SUPERMARKET - DAY   74

Will's buying prepackaged wealthy bachelor food -- prepared
risotto, reheatable crispy fragrant duck, etc. As he rounds
a corner we see MARCUS, tailing him, avoiding being seen.

Will looks down at his cart and notices a jar of PUREED
CHICKEN. Stops for a second. Thinks. Laughs at himself, as
though he's realized he subconsciously put it there for
"Ned". Takes out the jar and takes it back to the infant
section nearby. As he does, Marcus sneaks up and throws
something else into Will's cart.

LATER, At the CHECKOUT COUNTER, Will notices that the cashier
is checking out a package of NAPPIES.

                    WILL
                (confused)
            That's not mine.

Over his shoulder, we can see Marcus.

75   EXT. WILL'S FLAT - DAY   75

Will opens the door. For a moment, he looks into thin air.
Then he looks down and sees Marcus standing there.

                    MARCUS
            You don't have a kid, do you?

                    WILL
            What?

                    MARCUS
            I've been watching you, and you
            don't have a kid.

                    WILL
            Well...what's it to you?

                    MARCUS
            Nothing. Except you've been lying
            to me, and my Mum, and my Mum's
            friend.
                (pause)
            Can I come in?

                    WILL
            No, you can't.

                    MARCUS
            Why? What are you doing?

                    WILL
            Just...watching TV.

                    MARCUS
            I could watch it with you, if you
            want.

                    WILL
            That's very nice of you, Marcus,
            but I usually manage on my own.
            Haven't you got homework to do?

                    MARCUS
            Yeah. Do you want to help me?

                    WILL
          That wasn't what I meant. I meant,
          why don't you go home and do it?

                    MARCUS
          Alright, but I'm gonna tell my mum.

                    WILL
          Oooh, I'm scared.
               (V.O.)
          *That's the best I could come up
          with. "Ooh, I'm scared". But as a
          matter of fact, I was.*

                    MARCUS
          I'll do you a deal. I won't tell
          anybody you don't have a kid -- if
          you go out with my Mum.

                    WILL
          Why would you even want your mum to
          go out with somebody like me?

                    MARCUS
          Well, you're not too bad. I mean,
          you told lies, but apart from that
          you seem okay.

                    MARCUS (CONT'D)
          And she's sad, and I think she'd
          like a boyfriend.

                    WILL
          Marcus, I can't go out with someone
          just because you want me to. I'd
          have to like the person as well.

                    MARCUS
          What's wrong with her?

                    WILL
          Nothing's wrong with her, but --
          Listen, I really don't want to talk
          about this with you. Go home.

                    MARCUS
          OK. But I'll be back.

Marcus leaves.

```
                          WILL (V.O.)
                       (Closes the door)
                 When I joined SPAT, I imagined
                 beautiful young mums, not skilled
                 bounty-hunters who would be able to
                 track me back to my house.
```

76   EXT. WILL'S FLAT - DAY   76

        MATCH CUT to the door opening on Marcus. It's the next day.
        Marcus is in his school clothes. In the reverse shot we see
        Will standing there, dressed differently from the previous
        day.

        Will tries to SHUT THE DOOR on Marcus, but Marcus wedges his
        foot in. Will slides his foot out and closes the door.

77   EXT. GROCERY   STORE - DAY   77

        We see Will through the window of a grocery shop. As Marcus
        passes by in the street, Will notices him and DUCKS OUT OF
        SIGHT. Gets up slowly after Marcus clears frame.

78   EXT. WILL'S FLAT - DAY   78

        Marcus rings Will's doorbell. Leaves.

79   INT. WILL'S FLAT - DAY   79

        Next day. Will is listening to music.

80   EXT. WILL'S STREET - DAY   80

        Marcus walks down the street towards Will's flat.

81   EXT. WILL'S FLAT - DAY   81

        Marcus rings the doorbell.

82   INT. WILL'S FLAT - LIVING ROOM - DAY   82

        Will hears the doorbell ring, and TURNS UP THE MUSIC.

83   EXT. WILL'S FLAT - DAY   83

        Marcus starts RINGING THE DOORBELL IN TIME WITH THE MUSIC.

84   INT. WILL'S FLAT - DAY   84

        Will is driven crazy by the RINGING OF THE DOORBELL. He GETS
        UP.

85   EXT. WILL'S FLAT - DAY   85

Will opens to door. Looks at Marcus. Marcus still has his
finger poised by the bell, threateningly. Will submits.
Motions him in.

86   INT. WILL'S FLAT - SITTING ROOM - SAME   86

Will and Marcus sit watching TV. Will looks over
suspiciously at Marcus, who's intent on the programme. As
the show ends, Marcus gets up.

                        MARCUS
              Thanks. See ya.

Marcus reaches out his hand. Will shakes it. Marcus heads
out.

87   EXT. WILL'S FLAT - DAY   87

Marcus walks away from Will's place.

88   INT. WILL'S FLAT - SITTING ROOM - NEXT DAY   88

Will glances up from the TV at his trendy wall-clock. The
DOORBELL RINGS.

89   EXT. WILL'S FLAT - DAY   89

Marcus is there.

90   INT. WILL'S FLAT - SITTING ROOM - THE NEXT DAY   90

Will and Marcus sit watching TV. Will appears to be a little
less freaked by the whole situation. Then they LAUGH at the
same bit on TV. Will looks a little miffed, like he's given
in to the enemy.

91   EXT. WILL'S FLAT - NEXT DAY   91

Marcus walks up to Will's front door. He's about to ring the
doorbell when the DOOR OPENS. Will lets Marcus in, without
so much looking at him. Turns and heads into the flat as
Marcus follows him.

92   OMIT   92

93   OMIT   93

94   OMIT   94

95   INT. WILL'S FLAT - SITTING ROOM - DAY   95

Marcus and Will sit watching a quiz show on TV. Marcus
divides his attention between the TV and Will, who sits there
smoking.

                    MARCUS
          You shouldn't smoke, you know.

                    WILL
          Really? Wow, I didn't know.
          Thanks for telling me.

Marcus gets up and starts looking at Will's stuff.

                    MARCUS
          Will, you've got a nice flat.

                    WILL
          Thank you.

                    MARCUS
          Only one bedroom, though.

                    WILL
          Yeah, largely on account of the
          fact that I can only sleep in one
          bed at a time.

                    MARCUS
          But you could get a bigger place if
          you wanted to.

Marcus heads into the kitchen and fetches a coke from the
fridge.

                    WILL
          Would you like anything to drink,
          Marcus?

                    MARCUS
               (not getting the irony)
          Thanks, I just got a coke.

                    MARCUS (CONT'D)
          Who are these people on the wall?
          With the saxophones and the
          trumpets?

                    WILL
          Saxophonists and trumpeters.

                    MARCUS
          Yeah, but why are they on your
          wall?

                    WILL
          Because they're cool.

                    MARCUS
          What's cool about them?

                    WILL
          Probably that they took drugs and
          died, I guess.

CLOSE ON MARCUS. Takes this in. Will realizes what he's
said.

                    MARCUS
          Okay. I better get home. Thanks.

                    WILL
          Wait a second.
            (off Marcus's look)
          You may as well catch the beginning
          of Saved by the Bell.

Marcus shrugs and sits down again.

The we CUT TO JUMP CUTS of Will and Marcus on the same couch.
Marcus is in his school uniform, but Will is wearing a
different outfit each time (note to Joanna: don't freak out -
- it's okay to just recombine some previously used costumes
for Will). We are establishing the growing everydayness of
Marcus's visits by jump-cutting to them in slightly different
positions on the couch, different expressions, etc.

96   INT. SNOOKER HALL - DAY   96

Will is playing snooker, about to pot a ball when he realizes
something, checks his watch, and, making his apologies, heads
off...

97   INT. WILL'S FLAT - LATER THAT DAY   97

Will checks his watch again. Seems uncomfortable, a little
bereft that Marcus isn't there.

98   EXT. WILL'S FLAT - NEXT DAY   98

Will opens the door, Marcus is there. Will hides the fact
that he's pleased.

99   INT. WILL'S FLAT - DAY   99

Later, they sit on the couch, watching TV again.

                    WILL
             (casually)
          So...what happened yesterday?

                    MARCUS
             (shrugs)
          I had work to do.
             (pause)
          Did you go to school when you were
          a kid?

                    WILL
          Incredibly, Marcus, yes, I did.

                    MARCUS
          Why? I mean, you didn't really
          need to, did you? If you weren't
          going to get a job. You could have
          left school when you were six or
          seven. Saved yourself all the
          hassle.

                    WILL
          Good point.

                    MARCUS
          So why did you go?

                    WILL
          Well, my mum and dad forced me,
          didn't they?

Marcus thinks about this for a bit.

                    MARCUS
          What was your dad like?

                    WILL
          I dunno. Bit sad. Wrote one crap
          song which became a massive hit and
          spent the rest of his life trying
          to write a better one.

                    MARCUS
          So did you want to write songs too?
          Is that what the guitar's for?

                        WILL
          No. I Mean, yeah, I thought about
          it for a bit, but then it turned
          out all I could write was songs
          that were even more crap than my
          dad's, and since he wrote the most
          crap song in history, well, I just
          let it slide.

There's a pause.

                        MARCUS
          I like Santa's Super Sleigh. It
          makes people happy at Christmas.
          My mum says that music unites
          people. She says that when I sing,
          I bring joy and sunshine into her
          heart.

                        WILL
          Marcus, please. I just ate.

100   INT. WILL'S FLAT - ANOTHER DAY   100

Marcus and Will are again watching TV

                        MARCUS (V.O.)
          After I came visiting a while, Will
          seemed to think he had to ask me
          serious questions. But I knew he
          was more interested in watching the
          fat guy on TV.

                        WILL
          So...how are things going at home?

                        MARCUS
               (looks at Will, surprised)
          You mean my Mum?
               (trying to be casual)
          She's alright, thanks.

                        WILL
          No, you know, I mean...

                        MARCUS
          Yeah, I know. No, nothing like
          that.

                        WILL
          Does it still bother you?

                         MARCUS
                    Does it bother me?

101   OMIT   101

102   OMIT   102

103   INT. FIONA'S FLAT - STAIRWAY - LATE AFTERNOON   103

        WE SEE Marcus trudging up the stairs, and his distorted POV
        of the door opening, a woman slumped on the floor.

                         MARCUS (V.O.)
                    Every single day...

104   INT. WILL'S FLAT - SITTING ROOM - DAY (AS BEFORE)   104

                         MARCUS (V.O.)
                    That's why I come here instead of
                    going home.
                         (aloud)
                    A bit. When I think about it.

                         WILL
                         (seeing Marcus'
                         expression)
                    Fucking hell...

        Marcus looks over at Will.

105   EXT. WILL'S STREET - DUSK   105

        Marcus walks away from Will's flat. We see him walk down
        various streets.

                         MARCUS (V.O.)
                    I didn't know why he swore like
                    that, but it made me feel better.

                         MARCUS (V.O.) (CONT'D)
                    It made me feel like I wasn't being
                    pathetic to get so scared.

106   INT. ENTRANCE TO TRENDY SUPERMARKET - NIGHT   106

        Will walks into the fancy supermarket.

                         WILL (V.O.)
                    I wouldn't make the mistake of
                    asking about Fiona again.
                         (MORE)

> WILL (V.O.) (cont'd)
> *Marcus was clearly messed up about*
> *it, and unfortunately I couldn't*
> *think of anything to say that would*
> *be of the smallest value.*

107   INT. TRENDY SUPERMARKET - NIGHT   107

Will picks up risotto, some truffles, designer vegetables.
We hear a jingly, muzacky Christmas song on the supermarket
stereo system.

> WILL (V.O)
> *Next time, he could talk to Suzie,*
> *or a counsellor, or anybody capable*
> *of something more than an*
> *obscenity.*

The CHRISTMAS SONG RISES as Will notices it.

> WILL (CONT'D)
> (aloud)
> Shit! It can't be.

The song is SANTA'S SUPER SLEIGH.

> WILL (V.O.) (CONT'D)
> *November 19th. A new record. A*
> *month ahead of time, and they were*
> *already playing the damn song.*
> *That meant a whole damn month of*
> *listening to it.*

> SONG OVER LOUDSPEAKERS (V.O.)
> Ho ho ho -- hey hey hey, it's
> Santa's Super Sleigh!!!

As Will rounds an aisle, he sees a rumpled, grey haired man
in tweeds, slipping one of those drinks bottles so big they
have their own handle off the shelf. Dewar's.

> WILL
> Dad?

But then he's gone. Will keeps going.

108   INT. SCHOOL - DAY   108

Marcus, standing in the corridor at school, is looking at a
notice for an upcoming SCHOOL CONCERT. He looks up as ELLIE,
the punky-looking girl who we saw earlier, walks by.

> MARCUS
> (smiles)
> Hello.

                    ELLIE
              (same kind of smile)
         Fuck off.

Surprisingly, Marcus looks...intrigued. Then something HITS
Marcus on the back of the head, and goes clattering down the
corridor. Marcus turns and sees two older kids coming
towards him. He starts backing away from them.

109   INT. WILL'S FLAT - DAY   109

Will sits on his sofa, watching Countdown.

From outside, we hear KNOCKING -- not person-knocking-on-the-
door knocking, but HAILSTONE knocking, as though somebody
were throwing rocks at the house. This sound is shortly
followed by a frantic and persistent RINGING of the doorbell.

Will looks unsettled, frowns, and turns up the VOLUME on the
gameshow. But it's not high enough to drown out the CRACKLING
and RINGING.

110   EXT. WILL'S FLAT - DAY   110

The door opens to reveal a couple of mean-looking kids
throwing what appear to be geological samples but are in fact
hard candies at Marcus, who has been dodging them and ringing
the bell. Will shoves Marcus inside the flat.

                    WILL
              (to the kid)
         Oi! What do you think you are
         doing?

                    MEAN KID#1
         Who are you?

                    WILL
         Who am I? Bugger off, that's who I
         am!

                    MEAN KID#2
              (trying to act unscared)
         Oo-er.

But the two of them high-tail it immediately, leaving Will
looking a little pleased with himself.

111   INT. WILL'S FLAT - DAY   111

When Will comes back into the sitting room, eyeing a piece of
hard candy he's picked up from the ground, Marcus is sitting
on the couch, watching the game show, as though nothing had
happened.

                    WILL
          Who were they, then?

                    MARCUS
          Who?

                    WILL
          Who? The ones who were trying to
          embed sweets into your skull.

                    MARCUS
          Oh, them. They're just a couple of
          older kids. They just started
          following me after school.

                    WILL
          So does this happen often?

                    MARCUS
          They never chucked sweets before.
          They just thought of that one.

                    WILL
          I wasn't talking about the sweets.
          I'm talking about kids trying to
          kill you.

                    MARCUS
          Oh. Yeah.   They give me a hard
          time...You know, about my hair and
          my clothes and singing and stuff.

                    WILL
          ...Singing?

                    MARCUS
          Yeah. Sometimes I sing out loud
          without noticing it.

                    WILL
              (pause)
          Well, I can see that that's not a
          great idea.

MARCUS
I said I did it without noticing,
didn't I? It just happens. Do you
think I would do it on purpose?
I'm not stupid, you know.

WILL
Sorry. My advice is, stay out of
people's way. Try to be invisible.

MARCUS
(getting angry)
How am I supposed to be invisible?
Is one of the machines in your
kitchen an invisible machine? I
don't think so.
(pause)
I just try not to think of it,
that's all. It happens, and I wish
it didn't, but it's just life,
isn't it? There's nothing I can do
about it.

Will looks at Marcus, his annoyance with him subsiding. He
sits down facing Marcus, looking Marcus in the face, serious
and determined.

WILL
(heartfelt)
There is something we can do about
this, Marcus. You're coming with
me.

CUT TO:

112   INT. NIKETOWN - DAY   112

CLOSE ON a HIGH-TECH TRAINER (SNEAKER).

Marcus and Will stand there in Niketown, high-tech, air-
conditioned, Michael Jordan-endorsed mecca of cool footwear.
A cute salesgirl in fly gear sets down a few boxes of shoes
that share design features with Star Wars spaceships.

MARCUS
I don't get it.

WILL
We're starting with your feet,
Marcus. I can't make you
invisible, but I can make you blend
in with the crowd.

Marcus looks around at all the other shoppers milling about.

> MARCUS
> Sheep. Baaaaa.
> (beat)

> MARCUS (CONT'D)
> That's what Mum says when she
> thinks people haven't got a mind of
> their own.

> WILL
> The point of this whole expedition,
> Marcus, is to make you into a
> sheep. Baaa. So how do you like
> these ones?

Marcus has slipped on a pair of really cool Nikes.

> MARCUS
> They cost sixty pounds.

> WILL
> Never mind that.

> MARCUS
> I don't know how to tie them.
> They've got these weird straps.

> WILL
> It's a revolutionary technology
> called velcro, Marcus. There were
> a few deaths early on, but it's no
> longer dangerous now that the early
> prototypes have been refined.

Will looks at Marcus, who's still staring down at them.

> MARCUS
> They don't look dangerous.

> WILL
> Oh, for Christ's sake.

Will leans over and "ties" Marcus's shoes, or rather fastens them. It's actually a pretty funky arrangement of straps, and it takes Will a second to figure them out.

In the mirror, Will sees that the CUTE SHOPGIRL is looking at him. But she's got an oh-isn't-it-cute-to-see-a-father-tying-his-son's-shoes look. She musses Marcus's hair.

                         SHOPGIRL
                    (patronizing re Will)
             Your old man's pretty trendy, isn't
             he?

Will's smile freezes. He looks at himself in the mirror.
Sees the crow's feet around his eyes. Look up at Marcus, the
bloom on his cheeks. Sits there considering.

                         MARCUS
             I'm going to be late for school
             every morning if it takes this long
             to get them on.

                         WILL
             There. Locked and loaded.

Will stands up. Marcus starts stomping around, looking at
himself in the mirror. Trying to repress a smile.

                         WILL (CONT'D)
             You think you look cool, don't you?

                         MARCUS
             I don't know. Do you think I look
             cool?

                         WILL
             Yeah, Marcus. You look cool.

                         MARCUS
                    (pause; then, smiling)
             Yeah.

Marcus nods and smiles. He and Will head to the counter.

                         WILL (V.O)
             *I was suddenly hit by an
             extraordinary rush of well-being.
             So this was what people meant by a
             natural high -- and it only cost
             sixty pounds! I had made an
             unhappy boy temporarily happy. And
             there wasn't anything in it for me
             at all. I didn't even want to get
             into his mum's knickers.*

Will hands over his credit card at the REGISTER.

113   EXT. FIONA'S FLAT - DAY   113

A familiar frame by now -- the door opens to reveal Marcus.
He's standing there, crying. Behind him, it's raining.

FIONA (O.S.)
Marcus!

114   EXT. FIONA'S FLAT - SAME   114

We reveal that Marcus is not, in fact, standing in front of
Will's doorway but the doorway of his own house.

FIONA
My God, what happened to your
shoes?

We see that Marcus is wearing his socks, which are soaked
through in the pouring rain.

MARCUS
They stole them.

115   INT. FIONA'S FLAT - SAME   115

Fiona and Marcus sit, Marcus towelling his head dry while
Fiona dries his feet.

MARCUS (V.O.)
*I could see I was going to have to
tell the truth, but the problem was
that the truth was going to lead to
a lot more questions.*

FIONA
Why would anyone steal your shoes?

MARCUS
They were nice ones.

FIONA
But they were just ordinary black
loafers.

MARCUS
No they weren't. They were new
Nike Air Jordans.

FIONA
Where did you get new Nike --
whatevers from?

MARCUS
Will bought them for me.

FIONA
Will? The guy who took us to
lunch?

                    MARCUS
          Yeah. He's sort of become my
          friend.

                    FIONA
          He's sort of become your friend?

Marcus's next V.O. is over a silent shot of Fiona asking the
next logical question, something like, "what do you mean,
he's sort of your friend?"

                    MARCUS (V.O.)
          Yeah. She had loads more
          questions. She kept repeating the
          last thing I said, except she
          shouted it.
               (out loud)
          I go round to his place after
          school.

                    FIONA
          YOU GO ROUND TO HIS PLACE AFTER
          SCHOOL?

                    MARCUS
          Well, you see, he doesn't really
          have a kid.

                    FIONA
          HE DOESN'T REALLY HAVE A KID?

                    MARCUS
          Can I play computer games now,
          please?

A pause.

                    FIONA
          Where does he live?

                    MARCUS
          He's not there now, he's out to
          dinner -

Fiona grabs Marcus's hand and yanks him up --

116   OMIT   116

117   INT. TRENDY RESTAURANT - NIGHT   117

Will sits across the table from Christine, the mother-of-two
who we saw earlier in the movie.

They're at a table in the trendy restaurant where Will
brought Fiona and Marcus earlier.

                    WILL (V.O.)
          Christine had asked me out to
          dinner for one of her pep talks.

                    CHRISTINE
          ...You'll end up childless and
          alone.

                    WILL
          Well, hopefully, yes.

Christine looks at him, glares at him, in fact.

                    CHRISTINE
          Well, you must have a lot of
          courage.

                    WILL
          How's that?

                    CHRISTINE
          Most people...most people need
          something in their life to...well,
          to keep them afloat. But you, Will
          -- you've got absolutely nothing.
          It's very brave.

Will looks blanched.

A CUTE WAITRESS appears on the scene.

                    CUTE WAITRESS
          Do you know what you want?

Will looks up at the waitress, a little confused. Then notes
her cuteness. Smiles. She smiles back.

118   EXT. TRENDY RESTAURANT - NIGHT   118

As some trendy patrons exit Will's usual haunt, they're
surprised by Fiona crashing through the door in the opposite
direction, dragging Marcus --

119   INT. TRENDY RESTAURANT - NIGHT   119

                    FIONA (O.S.)
          Okay, now what the hell are these
          little after-school tea parties
          about?

Fiona is standing there, furious, with Marcus in tow.

                    WILL
          Fiona, Marcus...hi...sorry -- what?

                    FIONA
          I was just wondering why a single,
          childless man would want to hang
          out with a twelve-year-old boy
          every day?

Christine looks at Will. Something dawns on her...meanwhile,
the waitress is still standing there, taking in the scene.

                    WILL
          Are you suggesting what I think
          you're suggesting?

                    FIONA
          I'm not suggesting anything.

                    WILL
          You think I've been...fiddling with
          your son?

Patrons turn to observe the scene.

                    FIONA
          I'm simply asking why you entertain
          twelve-year-olds in your flat.

                    CHRISTINE
          Oh my God.

                    WAITRESS
          Oh my God.

                    FIONA
          What do you have to say for
          yourself? Well?

Will's had about enough of this. He leaps up.

                    WILL
               (exploding)
          Well? Well I don't have any
          choice, do I? Your son comes round
          uninvited every night! And you
          know why? Because he's having the
          shit bullied out of him and you
          haven't got a clue! You send him
          out there like a lamb to the
          slaughter! He's getting taken to
          pieces every day of the week, you
          daft fucking hippy!

                    FIONA
          I think you're being a bit
          melodramatic. Marcus is doing
          fine.

Marcus looks confused and, at the same time, tired. He sits
down at the table.

                    MARCUS (V.O.)
          It was strange. Will had it right,
          and Mum didn't. It was supposed to
          be the other way around.

                    FIONA
          Maybe you haven't had very much
          contact with kids before.

                    WILL
          I used to be a bloody kid. And I
          used to go to a bloody school.

                    WILL (CONT'D)
          I know the difference between kids
          who can't settle down and kids who
          are just plain miserable, so don't
          give me any crap about being
          melodramatic. I'm supposed to take
          this from someone who --

                    MARCUS
               (shouts)
          Ow! Cowabunga!

                    WILL
          What's wrong with you?

                    MARCUS
          Nothing, just...wanted to have a
          shout.

                    WILL
          Jesus. What a family.

A MAITRE D' has come up.

                    MAITRE D'
          Mr. Freeman...please...you're
          disturbing the other customers...

They all stand there for a second.

                         WILL
                    (to the Maitre d')
          It's fine. I'm done.

                         CHRISTINE
          Then...you're not gay?

                         WILL
          NO!
                    (to Fiona)
          Don't worry about it. I won't open
          the door to Marcus again. I'll be
          glad to be rid of the pair of you.
                    (to Marcus)
          Go on, then.

Marcus looks stricken. Fiona notices Marcus' look.

                         WILL (CONT'D)
          Well?

Suddenly Fiona sits down.

                         FIONA
          So that's it, is it? You're out of
          his life, just like that?

Will takes a moment to absorb this.

                         WILL
          Excuse me?

                         FIONA
          Let's say you're right, and I'm
          wrong.   Let's say there's this
          whole world going on for Marcus,
          that I don't understand, and you
          do. What are you going to do about
          it?

                         WILL
          Nothing, obviously. He's none of
          my business!

                         FIONA
          God, you're a selfish bastard.

                         CHRISTINE
          That's what I've been trying to
          tell him. He always puts himself
          first.

                    WILL
          But I'm on my own. There's just
          me. I'm not putting myself first,
          because there's nobody else.

                    FIONA
          Yes there is. There's Marcus. You
          can't just keep life out. No man
          is an island.

                    CHRISTINE
          She's right, you know.

                    CUTE WAITRESS
               (still there)
          Yeh. She is.

                    WILL
          No, she's not. I am an island.
          I'm a very cool island. I'm bloody
          Maui, okay?

                    FIONA
          What on earth are you talking
          about?

                    MARCUS
               (brightly)
          Do you want to come over for
          Christmas?

120 OMIT   120

121 EXT. LONDON BRIDGE - DAY   121

     Will walks along the bridge, alone, a bag of shopping in his
     hand. A THRONG of businessmen in grey suits walk the other
     direction.

                    WILL (V.O.)
          No, Marcus, I do not want to come
          over for bloody Christmas.

122 INT. VIDEO STORE - DAY (INTERCUT)   122

     We see Will walking along a wall of videos. Above his head,
     the label for the section he's in -- HORROR.

                    WILL (V.O.)
          I do not want to spend Christmas
          with Miss Granola Suicide and her
          freaky offspring.

From the store speakers, we hear SANTA'S SUPER SLEIGH playing. Will winces.

123   INT. WILL'S FLAT - DAY   123

Will sits watching videos, drinking a Belgian beer. We move in on Will as he watches the video.

> WILL(V.O.)
> *The way I see it, what you do with Christmas is kind of a statement about where you stand in life. I was going to spend this Christmas the way I usually did, watching videos and getting drunk and stoned.*

ON SCREEN, we see footage from James Whale's <u>The Bride of Frankenstein</u>. Frankenstein is momentarily welcome at the house of an old blind man.

> OLD BLIND MAN
> Before you came, I was alone. Now, I have a friend. It is bad to be alone!

> FRANKENSTEIN
> (grunting)
> <u>Alone...bad. Friend...good!</u>

Will takes this in..

124   OMIT   124

125   OMIT   125

126   INT. FIONA'S FLAT - DAY   126

Will sits uncomfortably with various members of Fiona's family. There's a nut roast on the table, with numerous veggie side dishes.

> WILL (V.O.)
> *The good news was, it wasn't just me and Fiona and Marcus. The bad news was, well...*
> (aloud)
> So you're Marcus' Dad?

> CLIVE
> Yeah, I guess so. And this is my girlfriend, Lindsey.

            WILL
Ah.

            CLIVE
And Lindsey's mum.

           LINDSEY
And how to you fit in, Will?

            WILL
I'm...a friend. Of Marcus. And
Fiona's.

           CLIVE
Does anybody mind if I roll a
joint?

Fiona gives him a sharp look. Clive puts away his rolling
papers.

         CLIVE (CONT'D)
Sorry.

Cut to LATER. Numerous presents have been opened. Including
the latest, a PENIS SHAPED CHOCOLATE.

           FIONA
        (laughs)
...Thank you, Lindsey...

Marcus has opened a set of woolly socks from his father.

          MARCUS
Thank you, Dad!

            WILL
This one's from me.

Marcus opens Will's present.

          MARCUS
Wow! Brilliant!
        (pause)
What is it?

            WILL
It's a CD. By Mystikal.
        (explains)
They're cool.

It is, in fact, a CD by Mystikal, an extremely hard-core rap
group.

                    FIONA
               (a little suspicious)
     What kind of music is Mystikal?

                    WILL
     It's sort of...world music.

                    MARCUS
               (reading the CD cover)
     Shake Ya Ass!

                    WILL
               (off Fiona's look)
     Actually, it's rap.

                    LINDSAY'S MUM
     Shake Ya Ass. Is he Moroccan?

                    FIONA
     I'm afraid we don't have a CD
     player.

                    MARCUS
     It's great anyway, though.

                    WILL
     I know you don't have a CD player.
     I got you one of those too.

Marcus opens the Discman Will wrapped for him too.

                    WILL (CONT'D)
     The great thing about it is that
     you can turn it loud enough to
     damage your hearing, without
     disturbing anybody else.

                    FIONA
     I've got something musical for you
     too, Marcus.

                    MARCUS
     Really? Brilliant!

                    WILL (V.O.)
     I had to hand it to the kid. He
     could be enthusiastic about some
     really crap presents. It was as if
     he didn't want to let anyone down.

Marcus opens a present, which is...

                    MARCUS
          Wow! A tambourine! Thanks, Mum!
               (turning to Will)
          Isn't that great, Will?

                    WILL
          ...Yeah, that'll come in handy.

                    FIONA
          I saw it in the shop, and thought,
          this'll be perfect. I thought
          maybe...you could perform at that
          school concert. You know, maybe
          get a pop group together, make some
          friends...

                    MARCUS
          ...maybe, Mum.

                    FIONA
               (hugs him)
          When you sing, it brings sunshine
          and happiness into my heart.

                    MARCUS
          Thanks, Mum. Open yours, Will.

Will opens Marcus's present for him. It's "THE SINGLE
PARENT'S HANDBOOK". Fiona looks at Marcus, surprised.

                    WILL
               (surprised)
          Marcus...is this a joke?

                    MARCUS
          Yeah.

                    WILL
               (beat)
          Not bad.

                    SUZIE (O.S.)
          Sorry I'm late. Have I missed
          everything?

Suzie walks in, with Megan in tow.

                    WILL
               (stands)
          Hello, Suzie. Hello, Megan!

                              SUZIE
                         (cold)
                    Hello, Will. Where's "Ned"? At
                    his "mum's" for Christmas?

The rest of the guests take in Suzie's frostiness. Will sits
down. He stand up again, trying to decide what to do. Then
he sits down again.

                              WILL
                    Perhaps I should go.

                              SUZIE
                    Going to pose as Santa and try to
                    shag some carol singers, are you?

                              LINDSEY'S MUM
                    Are you a professional Santa?! How
                    lovely!

                              WILL
                         (stands up again)
                    Right. Thanks, I'm off.

                              FIONA
                    Suzie has a right to express her
                    anger, Will.

                              WILL
                    Yes, and she's expressed it, and
                    now I have a right to go home.

Will starts to leave, everybody looking at him.

                              MARCUS
                    Wait!

Everybody suddenly turns to Marcus, even Will.

                              MARCUS (CONT'D)
                    He's my friend. I invited him. I
                    should be able to tell him when to
                    go home.

                              FIONA
                    I haven't told Will to leave,
                    Marcus. Suzie's angry with Will,
                    as she has every right to be, and
                    she's telling him so.

Marcus looks at Will. Will looks completely humiliated and
defeated.

                    WILL
She's right, Marcus. Leave it
alone.

                    MARCUS
All he did was make up a kid for a
couple of weeks. God, that's
nothing. So what? Who cares?
Kids at school do worse than that
every day.

                    FIONA
The point is, Marcus, that Will
left school a long time ago. He
should have grown out of making
people up by now.

                    MARCUS
It's not fair to gang up on him.
He's been a lot better behaved
since then. He got me trainers,
and he let me come by his house,
even if he didn't want me to. And
he knows what kids need.

                    FIONA
What? Expensive footwear and
obscene music? If there's
something you really need, we can
talk about it.

                    MARCUS
No we can't. Because it's not
really a discussion, it's an
argument, and you always win. Why
don't you just tell me what to do?

                    FIONA
Because I want you to think for
yourself.

                    MARCUS
Okay, I'm thinking for myself. And
I want Will to stay. I mean, it's
not like he's the only one who ever
did anything wrong.
You remember how we met Will? You
remember why? Because --

                    WILL
               (cutting him off)
          It's because you threw a bloody
          great loaf of bread at a duck's
          head and killed it, basically.

Suzie laughs, followed by Fiona.

                    FIONA
               (recovering)
          Excuse me? What's this about a
          duck?

                    MARCUS (V.O.)
          At first, I didn't know why he
          brought that up, but then I
          realized -- he didn't want mum to
          feel bad, just like I didn't want
          him to feel bad.
               (aloud)
          I think it was sick already. It
          looked pretty old...

                    CLIVE
               (laughing too)
          Well I'm lost...

                    LINDSEY'S MUM
          Are we having duck? Delicious!

     CUT TO

127   INT. FIONA'S DINING ROOM - DAY   127

Everyone sits around the table, eating a vegetarian nut-loaf.

                    WILL (V.O.)
          Of course, we were not having duck.
          Instead, we had something called
          nut-loaf, with parsnip gravy.

                    FIONA
          Before we eat, I just want to say a
          few words. It's easy to forget that
          there are other people less
          fortunate than us. Not everyone has
          friends or family, or wonderful
          food to eat...

Will casts a look at the nut-loaf.

FIONA (CONT'D)
...so in spite of how
commercialized and corporate this
holiday has become...

We fade out and back into Will's V.O.

WILL (V.O.)
As I sat there, I had a strange
feeling...

128   INT. MARCUS'S BEDROOM - NIGHT   128

Alone in his room, Marcus takes out the Discman, puts in the
disc...and hits PLAY. Smiles.

WILL (V.O.)
...I was enjoying myself. I'd
never really enjoyed Christmas
before...

129   INT. WILL'S LIVING ROOM - NIGHT   129

Will sits reading the Single Parent's Handbook. Smiles.

WILL (V.O)
My mother used to make me sing
"Santa's Super Sleigh" in front of
a collection of inebriated uncles
and aunts, just to get at my Dad, I
think.

130   INT. FIONA'S SITTING ROOM - NIGHT   130

Fiona tentatively takes a bite out of the penis-shaped
chocolate.

WILL (V.O)
But Christmas at Marcus's...well,
I'm ashamed to say it gave me a
warm fuzzy feeling. And I held
that feeling directly responsible
for the disaster that followed.

131   INT. POSH FLAT - NIGHT   131

The cacophony of a big dinner party. It's New Year's Eve.
Will is sitting at a dinner table jammed full of attractive,
successful people. He is engaged in conversation with a very
attractive woman, RACHEL, about thirty-five, sitting to his
left.

                    WILL (V.O.)
*On New Year's Eve, something
terrible happened. Something I'd
taken scrupulous care to avoid all
my life. I fell in love.*

The rest of Will's VO occurs over what seems to be a normal
conversation of two people attracted to one another, but
which filmically has the feel of something going wrong. More
like a suspense film than anything else.

                  WILL (V.O.) (CONT'D)
*Her name was Rachel. She was a
cartoonist. She was interesting
and smart and attractive. And for
about five minutes, I had her
convinced that I was too.*

                  RACHEL
Quite how I came to spend my whole
life drawing pictures of frogs
discussing political events, I'll
never know. You're in television,
right?

                  WILL
No. I do <u>watch</u> a lot of it.

                  RACHEL
I see. So you're more <u>in front</u> of
television than <u>in</u> it.

                  WILL
Yes. Although I did have a terrible
nightmare the other day where I
actually was <u>in</u> the television. It
was pretty cramped.

In fact, Rachel does seem to be interested. Will, though, is
starting to get the look of a swimmer running out of energy,
about to plunge beneath the surface.

                  WILL (CONT'D)
*Her name was Rachel. She was a
cartoonist. She was interesting
and smart and attractive. And for
about five minutes, I had her
convinced that I was too.
It was torture. For five minutes I
realized what life would be like if
I were in any way interesting; if I
had anything to say for myself, if
I did anything.*
                (MORE)

                    WILL (CONT'D)
          But I didn't do anything. And in
          about thirty seconds she would
          know...and she'd be gone like a
          shot.

We rejoin their conversation.

                    RACHEL
          ...So if you're not a TV mogul, how
          do you know Richard?

                    WILL
          Uh...just...I bought my dope off
          him years ago.

                    RACHEL
               (pause)
          Oh. Right. Well, that's great.
          Drugs really...bring people
          together, don't they? I mean. At
          least the two of you have kept in
          touch.

                    WILL
          Yeah. Dunno why, really.

                    RACHEL
          So, what do you do?

                    WILL
          Well, I'm sort of...taking some
          time off right now.

                    RACHEL
          Oh. Sounds great.

                    WILL
               (momentarily relieved)
          Yeah...

                    RACHEL
               (interested)
          Time off from what?

                    WILL
          Uh, well, time off from...time off,
          actually. See...the interesting
          thing...the interesting thing is, I
          don't...do anything.

                    RACHEL
          You don't do anything?

                    WILL
     Actually, no.

                    RACHEL
     Nothing.

                    WILL
     No.

                    RACHEL
     Wow.

There's a pause, and Rachel's tablemate to her left attracts
her attention. Will sits there, looking forlorn.

                    WILL
     Her name was Rachel. She was a
     cartoonist. She was interesting
     and smart and attractive. And for
     about five minutes, I had her
     convinced that I was too.
     It was torture. For five minutes I
     realized what life would be like if
     I were in any way interesting; if I
     had anything to say for myself, if
     I did anything. But I didn't do
     anything. And in about thirty
     seconds she would know...and she'd
     be gone like a shot. There. She
     was gone. There was no more to
     say.

                    RACHEL
          (to other tablemate)
     I know this makes me a useless old
     bag, but all rap music sounds the
     same to me.

                    WILL (V.O.)
     ...or was there?
          (interrupting Rachel's
          conversation)
     I know a twelve year old who'd kill
     you for saying that.

                    RACHEL
     So do I, come to that. Maybe they
     should meet. What's yours called?

                    WILL
     Mine? Well...

As Will considers, we hear the tick-tock theme music from
COUNTDOWN.

                    WILL (CONT'D)
          He's called Marcus.

                    RACHEL
          Mine's Ali. Alistair.

                    WILL
          Right.
               (V.O.)
          Her name was Rachel. She was a
          cartoonist. She was interesting
          and smart and attractive. And for
          about five minutes, I had her
          convinced that I was too.
          It was torture. For five minutes I
          realized what life would be like if
          I were in any way interesting; if I
          had anything to say for myself, if
          I did anything. But I didn't do
          anything. And in about thirty
          seconds she would know...and she'd
          be gone like a shot. There. She
          was gone. There was no more to
          say.And there it was. It wasn't a
          lie. It was 100% her assumption.
          Well, 50% at the very least.

                    RACHEL
          And is Marcus into rap, and
          skateboards, and the Lara Croft,
          and all of that?

Will raises his eyes to the skies and chuckles fondly.

                    WILL
          <u>Is</u> he...

132   INT. SAME - LATE   132

The countdown to midnight and the New Year. We're in the
living room now, crowds milling about, people looking for the
people they want to kiss. Will walks up the stairs from one
part of the party to another, looking for Rachel.

                    WILL(V.O.)
          Her name was Rachel. She was a
          cartoonist. She was interesting
          and smart and attractive. And for
          about five minutes, I had her
          convinced that I was too.
               (MORE)

                    WILL(V.O.) (cont'd)
*It was torture. For five minutes I
realized what life would be like if
I were in any way interesting; if I
had anything to say for myself, if
I did anything. But I didn't do
anything. And in about thirty
seconds she would know...and she'd
be gone like a shot. There. She
was gone. There was no more to
say.And there it was. It wasn't a
lie. It was 100% her assumption.
Well, 50% at the very least.I was
in fantasy land again. But this
time it was different. SPAT was for
fun. This was serious. I was in
love, and my whole life was riding
on it. I acted in self defense.*

                    THE CROWD
Ten...nine...eight...seven...

                    WILL (V.O.)
*We arranged to get our lads
together. Which means we arranged
for us to get together. Single
parents, alone together.*

Will is still searching...

                    THE CROWD
Six...five...four...three...two...
one...

A tap on his shoulder. Rachel is there.

                    RACHEL
Happy New Year.

She leans towards him, tentatively...they kiss, lightly.

                    WILL (V.O.)
I was in serious trouble.

Will and Rachel lean back from each other...he looks at her.
The look is a mix of excitement, and fear.

133   INT. SCHOOL - DAY   133

We see some COOL KIDS, including ALI, a large 12 year old,
walking along the corridor. Ellie, the punked out kid, comes
from the opposite direction, carrying a guitar case. From
the way that people clear a path for Ellie and her lot, it's
obvious that she's pretty high in the pecking order.

As Marcus passes by a sign-up sheet for the SCHOOL CONCERT, we see that he is shaking his head and singing along to a rap song, namely Shake Ya Ass. He's lost in his own little headphone enclosed world.

                    MARCUS
               (raps)
          Shake Ya Ass -- but watch yo'self!
          Shake Ya Ass -- show me what you
          workin' with!

Ellie stops dead.

                    ELLIE
          Oi, titch! What did you just say
          to me?

                    MARCUS
          Shake Ya --

Marcus stops, sees himself face to face with Ellie, her cool friends gathered around. Marcus takes off his headphones, looks questioningly.

                    ELLIE
          You heard me, you squitty shitty
          little snot-nosed bastard.

                    MARCUS
          No I didn't. Sorry. I was just
          singing along to this song. By
          Mystikal. It's rap.

Ellie looks him up and down. Marcus has on a t-shirt for the band Badly Drawn Boy.

                    ELLIE
          You like rap?

                    MARCUS
          A little. It's by black people,
          mostly, and they're pretty angry,
          most of the time, but sometimes
          they just want to have sex.

This provokes laughter from the cool kids. Ellie scrutinizes him.

                    ELLIE
          Are you taking the piss? Because
          if you are, you'll get such a slap.

                         MARCUS
          I'm not taking the piss. I don't
          even know how to take the piss.

Again the cool kids laugh. Marcus laughs too. Ellie looks
confused.

                         ELLIE
          What's your name then?

                         MARCUS
          Marcus.

                         ELLIE
               (pause; then)
          I'm Ellie.

                         MARCUS
          Nice to meet you, Ellie.

Marcus holds out his hand.

                         ELLIE
          Not so fast. I'm not ready for
          physical contact yet. Next thing
          you know we'll be having sex. And
          where would that get us?

Marcus blushes. Ellie heads off, the cool kids eyeing Marcus
differently than before.

                         ELLIE (CONT'D)
               (turns)
          And stop telling strangers to shake
          their arse.

                         MARCUS
               (happy)
          Okay, Ellie! Seeya!

Marcus puts his headphones back on and walks to class. We see
that the student population in general is looking at Marcus a
little differently. He still sings along with the song, only
omitting the word "Ass" now.

                         MARCUS (CONT'D)
          Shake Ya -- mmmph --but watch
          yo'self! Shake Ya -- mmmph -- Show
          me what you're workin' with!

134   EXT. FIONA'S FLAT - DAY   134

Will RINGS on Fiona's/Marcus's doorbell. No response. He
LEANS on the buzzer, Marcus-style. Marcus opens the door,
looking quizzical.

                    WILL
          Marcus, I need your help.

135   EXT. ZOO - DAY   135

We join Marcus and Will walking in the zoo.

                    WILL (V.O.)
          I took him to the zoo, scene of my
          past kid triumph.

                    MARCUS
          What are we doing here?

                    WILL
          What do you mean? The zoo's a
          treat. I thought you liked
          animals.

                    MARCUS
          Not particularly.
               (pause)
          Why did you tell this lady that I
          was your son?

                    WILL
          I didn't tell her. She just got
          the wrong end of the stick.

                    MARCUS
          So just tell her she got the wrong
          end of the stick.

                    WILL
          No.

                    MARCUS
          Why not?

                    WILL
          We're going around in circles here,
          Marcus. Just accept the facts,
          okay? You're my son.

                    MARCUS
          I'll tell her, if you like. I
          don't mind.

                    WILL
          That's very kind of you, Marcus,
          but no.

                    MARCUS
          Why not?

                    WILL
          Oh, for Christ's sake! Because she
          has this rare disease, and if she
          believes something that's not right
          and you tell her the truth, her
          brain will boil in her head and
          she'll die.

                    MARCUS
          That's a load of shit.

                    WILL
          Marcus...you just said "shit".

                    MARCUS
          Yeah.

They're in front of the MONKEY CAGE. Will tries to catch
Marcus's eye, but he's concentrating on the monkeys.

                    WILL
          Marcus...listen. I'm really
          interested in this woman.

                    MARCUS
          What do you mean, "interested"?
          What's so interesting about her?

                    WILL
          Okay. Here, Marcus. Here's my
          last scrap of dignity. Enjoy it. I
          want to go out with her. I'd like
          her to be my girlfriend.

Marcus turns from the cage, his eyes alight with pleasure.

                    MARCUS
          Ohhhhhh...brilliant! Why didn't
          you just say that?

                    WILL
          I -- never mind.

                    MARCUS
          There's this girl at school...
          Ellie.
                    (MORE)

                         MARCUS (cont'd)
               I kind of want her to be my
               girlfriend. At least, I think so.
               I've been meaning to ask you.
               What's the difference between a
               girl who's your friend, and a
               girlfriend?

                         WILL
               Well...do you want to touch her?

                         MARCUS
               Is that so important?

                         WILL
               Well, yeah, Marcus. You've heard
               about sex, right? It's kind of a
               big deal.

                         MARCUS
               I know, I'm not stupid. I just
               can't believe there's nothing more
               to it. I mean...I want to be with
               her more. I want to be with her
               all the time. And I want to tell
               her things, which I don't even tell
               you, or Mum. And I don't want her
               to have another boyfriend. If I
               could have those things, I wouldn't
               mind if I touched her or not.

                         WILL
                    (shakes his head)
               I tell you, Marcus, you'll learn.
               You won't feel like that forever.

     They walk on.

                         WILL (V.O.) (CONT'D)
               But later that night, when I was on
               my own...

136   INT. WILL'S FLAT - NIGHT   136

     Will sits on his couch, listening to music, LOUD. It's a
     song expressing deep, painful longing.

                         WILL (V.O.)
               ...I remembered the deal Marcus was
               prepared to strike. Yes, I wanted
               to touch Rachel. But right
               now...if I had the choice, I would
               settle for the less and the more
               that Marcus wanted.
                    (MORE)

WILL (V.O.) (cont'd)
Jesus, was I turning into Marcus?
Would he be buying me shoes soon?

137   EXT. STREET - HOLLAND PARK - DAY   137

Marcus and Will stand in front of the door of Rachel's very
nice house.

                    WILL
          Did you have to dress like that?

                    MARCUS
          Like what?

                    WILL
          Never mind. Just try to act
          normal, okay?

Will rings the doorbell.

                    MARCUS
          Wait. How much did I weigh at
          birth?

                    WILL
          I don't know, it was your birth.

                    MARCUS
          Yeah, but you should know,
          shouldn't you? If you're my dad, I
          mean.

                    WILL
          Marcus, she doesn't suspect we're
          not father and son, she's not going
          to be trying to catch us out.
               (pause)
          Okay, when's your birthday?

                    MARCUS
          August the 19th. What's my
          favorite food?

                    WILL
          Duck?

                    MARCUS
          Wrong. Spaghetti with mushroom
          sauce that my mum makes. So who's
          my Mum?

                    WILL
          Sorry?

                         MARCUS
                Who's my Mum?

                         WILL
                ...Your Mum's your Mum.

                         MARCUS
                So you were married to my Mum and
                you've split up.

                         WILL
                Yeah. Whatever.

                         MARCUS
                And does it bother you? Or me?

They look at each other. The situation is so weird that
Marcus starts LAUGHING, a particularly high-pitched and
inhuman MIAOW. Will can't help it; starts laughing too.

                         WILL
                    (laughing)
                It doesn't bother me. Does it
                bother you?

But Marcus is too busy laughing to reply. Will joins him
again. The door opens, and the two of them stop, like
they've been caught out. But they're still smiling. Rachel
looks at them bemusedly.

                         RACHEL
                Hi, Will! And it's...Mark, is that
                right?

                         MARCUS
                Marcus.

Will's smile fades.

                         WILL (V.O.)
                That one sentence was enough to
                send it all crashing down.

                         RACHEL
                C'mon in.

138   INT. RACHEL'S FLAT - DAY   138

We're on Will's face as he takes the place in. Warm,
inviting, sepia toned photos, etc. Etc.

                         WILL (V.O.)
                    Mark? How could she forget one
                    single detail of our conversation
                    on New Year's Eve? Clearly she had
                    not spent the last ten days
                    thinking and dreaming of me. I
                    remembered everything about her.
                    And I could never have forgotten
                    her kid's name --

                         RACHEL
                    (shouting)
               Ali? ALI?
                    (pause)
               Let's just go up.

Still leading Will, this time up the stairs.

                         WILL (V.O.)
                    That would be like forgetting when
                    England had won the World Cup, or
                    the real name of Luke Skywalker's
                    father. Mark, Marcus...it was all
                    the same to her. This was what I
                    had been afraid of. Devastation.
                    Pain. Loneliness. Sudden loony
                    mood swings. And now it was too
                    late.
                    (aloud)
               Lovely place.

Rachel knocks on Ali's door.

139   INT. ALI'S ROOM - DAY   139

ALI, a cool kid in baggy trousers, a head taller than Marcus,
opens the door. The place is definitely a teenager's den.
Alan Iverson, Gisele Bundchen, Rage Against the Machine. Ali
looks Will and Marcus up and down. Not impressed.

                         RACHEL
               Ali, Marcus. Marcus, Ali.

Marcus reaches his hand out. Ali shakes, ironically.

                         ALI
               You're in my year. At school.

                         MARCUS
               Oh, really? Yeah, I think I've
               seen you.

                         RACHEL
              Good, then you guys will have a lot
              to talk about. Ali, this is Will.
              Will, Ali.

Ali looks him up and down.

                         WILL
                    (trying to be cool)
              Awright?

                         ALI
              Awright?

                         RACHEL
              Do you guys want to hang out up
              here for a while?

Marcus looks to Will. Will nods.

                         MARCUS
              Okay.

                         WILL (V.O.)
              For a moment, I loved him. Really
              loved him.

Rachel and Will leave the room, Marcus standing there. Ali
just looks at him a few seconds. Marcus smiles
uncomfortably. Is about to speak --

                         ALI
              There's no fucking way.

                         MARCUS
                    (confused)
              ...No?

                         ALI
              I tell you, if your Dad goes out
              with my Mum you're dead. Really.
              Dead.

                         MARCUS
              Oh, he's all right.

                         ALI
              I don't care if he's all right. I
              don't want him going out with my
              Mum. So I don't want to see him or
              you around here ever again, okay?

                    MARCUS
          Well, I'm not sure it's really up
          to me.

                    ALI
          It better be. Or you're going to
          die.

                    MARCUS (V.O.)
          I was beginning to get the feeling
          that maybe this kid Ali was a
          serial killer.
               (trying to change the
                subject)
          Can I have a go on the computer?
          What games have you got?

                    ALI
          Are you listening to me?

                    MARCUS
          Yes, but I'm not sure there's very
          much I can do at the moment. Will --
          that's my Dad, I call him Will
          because -- well, anyway, he likes
          your Mum, and I think she's keen on
          him --

                    ALI
               (screaming)
          SHE'S NOT KEEN ON HIM! SHE'S ONLY
          KEEN ON ME!

140   INT. RACHEL'S SITTING ROOM - DAY   140

Will and Rachel sit together on the sofa, talking.

                    WILL (V.O.)
               (over Rachel's animated
                talk)
          One of the amazing things about
          Rachel was that I wanted to kiss
          her every time she was talking
          about something interesting. Which
          was all the time. It was sexy. It
          was weird.

We check back in on Rachel.

                              RACHEL
              I mean nowadays most cartoonists
              just use Adobe photoshop and email
              j-peg files to the newspaper, but
              I'm really old fashioned, I still
              just use India ink and Bailey Board
              -- Will, are you listening?

                              WILL
                    (surprised in his reverie)
              Yes, I am.

Rachel smiles at him and gives him a bemused look.

                              WILL (CONT'D)
              What?

                              RACHEL
              Nothing, it's just...you looked so
              much like Marcus just then.

                              WILL
              I did?

                              RACHEL
              Yeah. I think it's sweet how much
              he takes after you. And the way he
              dresses like you...

Will seems put off.

                              WILL
              I don't dress like Marcus.

                              RACHEL
              There! You just did that thing he
              does! That little head waggle!

Will seems nonplussed, but it's actually a tender moment.
They're leaning in towards one another when --

We hear a STOMPING as something whizzes by, and we hear the
door slam. Rachel goes to the door, looks out, comes back.

                              WILL
              Suddenly I didn't want her to step
              away, even for that long. It hurt,
              in my chest. What the hell was
              going on?

                              RACHEL
              I think Marcus has gone home.

141   EXT. - RACHEL'S STREET   - DAY   141

Marcus is walking down the street. Will runs up to him.

>   WILL
>   C'mon. We're going back.

>   MARCUS
>   He's off his head.

>   WILL
>   No, he's not.

>   MARCUS
>   He said he'd cut me up in little
>   bits and hide me under the
>   floorboards.

>   WILL
>   He did?

>   MARCUS
>   No...but I think he's capable of
>   it.

Will grabs Marcus's hand and drags him off.

>   WILL
>   C'mon. It'll be different. You'll
>   love it. I promise.

142   INT. RACHEL'S SITTING ROOM - DAY   142

Ali stands there, blubbering like a three-year-old child, in
front of Marcus, who looks immensely pleased.

>   RACHEL
>   Marcus, Ali has something to say to
>   you, doesn't he?

>   ALI
>   (snivelling)
>   Sorry, Marcus. I didn't mean to
>   say those things.

>   MARCUS
>   That's okay, Ali.

Ali reaches out his hand to shake. Marcus takes it. They
shake for what seems a little too long. Rachel laughs.

>   RACHEL
>   Ali finds all this very difficult.

                         WILL
              So does Marcus. You feel about the
              same, don't you?
                   (off Marcus's confusion)
              You know...having divorced
              parents...not knowing what to feel
              about new people...

                         MARCUS
              Oh. Yes. Absolutely. That's
              absolutely the way I feel.

                         RACHEL
              Ali didn't get along with the last
              guy I --

                         ALI
              He was a liar.

                         RACHEL
              Well...he wasn't one hundred
              percent good news. And I'm not
              saying, you know, that you and I,
              we're --

                         MARCUS
              Oh, it's okay. He fancies you. He
              told me.

     Will blanches.

143   EXT. NEWSAGENTS - DAY   143

     Marcus is listening to his Discman, looking at a copy of a
     Will-ish type magazine (GQ, Loaded, etc.) outside the local
     newsagents.

     Marcus finds himself HUMMING with the Discman. The song is
     "Killing me Softly".

                         MARCUS
                   (singing)
              I FELT ALL FLUSHED WITH FEVER,
              EMBARRASSED BY THE CROWD...I FELT
              HE FOUND MY LETTERS, AND READ EACH
              ONE ALOUD...

     We hear LAUGHTER, and suddenly Marcus is surrounded by Lee
     Hartley and his mates.

                         LEE HARTLEY
              Oi! What you singing, Fuzzy?

But Marcus just stands there, looking ahead of him. Lee
takes the Discman out of Marcus's hands.

                    LEE HARTLEY (CONT'D)
          Mind if I borrow this?

                    MARCUS
          Yes.

                    LEE HARTLEY
               (listening)
          Jesus. This is crap.

                    MARCUS
          Can I have that back please? It
          was a Christmas present and --

                    LEE'S MATE
          Fuck off.

                    ELLIE (O.S.)
          Oi!

Suddenly Ellie hooves into view.

                    ELLIE (CONT'D)
          You pathetic little shitbags. Give
          it back or you'll get such a slap.

Lee hands Marcus back the CD player, but Ellie SLAPS him
anyway, a nice ripe slap that raises the blood in his face.

                    ELLIE (CONT'D)
          Tricked you. Now run along, all of
          you, before I get really cross.

                    LEE HARTLEY
          Slag!

But Lee says it as he's walking away.

                    ELLIE
          Now, why does hitting someone make
          me a slag, I wonder? Boys are
          peculiar creatures. Not you,
          though, Marcus. Well, you're
          peculiar, but in a different way.

But Marcus is just staring at her, amazed. Ellie starts
walking, and Marcus follows her.

                    ELLIE (CONT'D)
Are you a little slow, Marcus? In
the head?

                    MARCUS
No. I'm not slow. I'm just funny.
That's what everybody tells me.

                    ELLIE
What were you singing, anyway?

                    MARCUS
Killing Me Softly.

                    ELLIE
     (ironically)
Wow. Well cool.

                    MARCUS
You think so?

                    ELLIE
Yeah. You should perform it at the
school concert. You'd become a
rock star. Before you know it,
it'd be Marky Marcus -- money,
women, drugs, then the gradual
slide into debauchery.

                    MARCUS
     (thinks)
I don't think so. I think people'd
make fun of me.

Ellie laughs and ruffles Marcus's hair in what is very
obviously a very older-sisterly gesture. Marcus clearly
takes it a different way, or wants to.

144   INT SNOOKER HALL   - DAY   144

Marcus and Will are playing snooker. Marcus is excitedly
describing Ellie's rescue of him from Lee Hartley and his
mates while they play.

                    MARCUS
You should have seen her!

                    WILL
I feel as though I did. So, things
are going really well with me and
Rachel --

                    MARCUS
Wham!

                    WILL
Yes. Wham. Like you said.

                    MARCUS
She's fantastic.

                    WILL
Yes, but...I'm not sure that it'll
be so easy for Ellie to think of
you as a boyfriend if she has to
turn into Mike Tyson [Alt: The
Rock] to defend you all the time.

                    MARCUS
Who's Mike Tyson?

                    WILL
Never mind. All I'm saying is, be
careful. This looks more like pet
and owner than boyfriend and
girlfriend.

                    MARCUS
So? At least I'm honest.

                    WILL
What do you mean?

                    MARCUS
Well, I mean, you and Rachel...

He gives an elaborate shrug.

                    WILL
What. What does --
     (repeats the shrug)
Mean?

                    MARCUS
     (thinking aloud)
Well, it's just that I think
there's a problem with you and
Rachel. I mean, you want to be
with her, but she thinks you have a
son. And you don't.

                         MARCUS (CONT'D)
          Now, if you're going to be with
          somebody, shouldn't you tell them
          things like that? I mean like...
          you know...the truth?

Will snorts, like Marcus has said something childish and not
to the point. Then he thinks.

145   OMIT   145

146   INT. TRENDY ASIAN RESTAURANT - NIGHT   146

Will and Rachel sit over dinner.

                         WILL (V.O.)
          So I told her the truth.

Rachel is listening.

                         WILL (V.O.) (CONT'D)
          *That I wasn't Marcus's natural
          father.*

                         RACHEL
          Oh.

Rachel looks a little confused, a piece of seaweed poised in
her chopsticks.

                         WILL (V.O.)
          *The problem is, once I told the
          truth, I knew there would be more
          questions.*
                    (out loud, changing
                     subjects)
          It's not really seaweed, you know.

                         RACHEL
                    (still confused)
          So -- sorry, I'm being a bit thick
          here -- if you're not Marcus's
          natural father, and you don't live
          with him, then how is he, you know,
          your son?

                         WILL
          Yes. Ha ha. I see what you mean.
          It must look very confusing from
          the outside.

                         RACHEL
          Tell me how it is on the inside.

                        WILL
          Oh, I don't know, it's just one of
          those things. So do you want to
          move onto wine now? Maybe some
          Chinese rice wine?

                   WILL (CONT'D)
               (peers at a menu, tries
                to pronounce:)
          Xiao...Xing?
               (pause; off Rachel's look)
          Anyway, tell me about your
          relationship with Ali. Is it as
          complicated as mine and Marcus's?

                        RACHEL
          No. I slept with his father and
          nine months later I gave birth, and
          that's about it. Pretty
          straightforward, but these things
          usually are.

                        WILL
          Yes, I envy you.

                        RACHEL
          I'm sorry to harp on this, but I
          still haven't got all this worked
          out. You're Marcus's stepfather,
          but you don't live with him or his
          mother.
               (pause)
          Did you ever live with Marcus's
          mother?

                        WILL
          Define "live with".

                        RACHEL
          Did you ever have a spare pair of
          socks at her house? Or a
          toothbrush? Were you in fact ever
          married to her? Have you ever had
          a romantic relationship with her?

Will's back is against the wall.

                        WILL
          ...No.

Will pops a spring roll in his mouth, and makes a big deal
out of chewing it, like it'll prevent conversation forever.
But Rachel just waits there.

                    WILL (CONT'D)
          I never actually said he was my
          son. The words, "I have a son
          called Marcus" never escaped my
          lips. That's what you chose to
          believe.

                    RACHEL
          Yeah, right, it's me that's the
          fantasist. I wanted to believe you
          had a son, so I let my imagination
          run riot.

                    WILL
          Well, I did play some part in it --

                    RACHEL
             (angry)
          No. Not at all. I met you and
          thought, cute guy, if only he had a
          kid, a geeky, teen-age son, if
          possible, and then you turned up
          with Marcus at my house, and bingo!
          I made this crazy link because of
          some deep psychological need in me!

                    WILL
          You shouldn't beat yourself up
          about it. Could have happened to
          anyone.

Rachel just looks at him.

                    RACHEL
          You know...the first time I met
          you...I thought you were a
          little...blank. And then you
          changed my mind. But...maybe I was
          right.

                    WILL
          The thing is...Rachel, I...It's a
          long...
             (then, defeated)
          I'm sorry, Rachel. You're right.
          I'm a...I'm really...nothing. I
          don't know what I was thinking.
          I'm sorry. Sorry.

Will gets up, and walks from the table, out the door...away.

147   INT. WILL'S FLAT - NIGHT   147

Will sits in his flat. The lights are on. The TV's on,
muted, with the stereo playing.

As he sits there, time passes, and all the lights go out,
leaving him in the lone remaining light. Then daylight
rises.

148   EXT. SCHOOL EXIT - DAY   148

As Marcus leaves school, he sees Ellie.

                    MARCUS
              Night, Ellie!

                    ELLIE
              Marcus! My man!

Ellie smiles at him, and walks past. A couple of other kids
have seen the interaction.

                    SIMON
              Bye, Marcus!

                    SECOND KID
              See ya, Marcus!

149   INT. FIONA'S HOUSE - LATER   149

Fiona, sitting on the couch, CRYING. A hell of a lot
reminiscent of when we saw her crying before her suicide
attempt.

Marcus comes in, a hop in his step. He turns the corner to
see Fiona.

She doesn't see him, but he's watching her. There's a look
of fear on his face.

                    MARCUS
              Mum?
                  (pause)
              Mum?

No response.

150   INT. WILL'S HOUSE - DAY   150

Will sits or rather slumps on his couch, listening to some
music. He's unshaven, looks like shit.

We hear RINGING on the doorbell. Will ignores it. But the ringing doesn't stop. Will turns off the stereo with his remote, gets up

151   EXT. WILL'S FLAT - DAY   151

Will opens the door. Marcus is there.

                    WILL
               (pause)
          ...Hi.

Marcus squeezes past him. Will waits a beat at the door, then closes it.

152   INT. WILL'S FLAT - DAY   152

He joins Marcus inside his flat.

                    MARCUS
          My Mum's at it again.

                    WILL
          ...At what?

                    MARCUS
          What do you mean, what? The
          crying. She just sits in the house
          all day, crying. In the morning,
          too.

                    WILL
          Oh...

                    MARCUS
          It's the same now as it was before
          she...you know. Before the Dead
          Duck Day.

Marcus looks at Will.

                    WILL
          Marcus, I'm...busy right now.

                    MARCUS
          You're busy?

Will nods.

                    MARCUS (CONT'D)
               (with disbelief)
          Doing what?

Will is blank.

                    MARCUS (CONT'D)
Didn't you hear me?

                    WILL
Yes...I heard you...what do you
want me to do about it?

                    MARCUS
I don't know. You could talk to
her.

                    WILL
And say what?

                    MARCUS
...I don't know.

                    WILL
Why should she listen to me? Who
am I to her? Nobody.

                    MARCUS
You're not nobody, you're...

                    WILL
Who? Who do you think I am? Who
do you think you are? You come
here, uninvited, you...disturb my
life, you screw things up for
me...what do you want from me,
Marcus? This is not my problem!
I'm not your family! I'm not your
uncle, I'm not your big brother,
and I think it's been established
that I'm not your bloody father!

Marcus shifts.

                    MARCUS
But --

                    WILL
Marcus, I'm...I'm a guy who can
tell you what trainers and records
to buy. That's it. But I can't
help you with real things. I can't
help with anything that means
anything.

                    MARCUS
You could try.

Will is silent.

                    MARCUS (CONT'D)
          You're right. You can't help me.
          How could you? All you do is sit
          around all day and watch telly and
          buy things, and you don't give a
          shit about anybody and nobody gives
          a shit about you.

Will doesn't say anything.

Marcus turns and leaves. Heads out the door. Will watches
him.

Goes back to the couch.

Takes out the remote.

153   EXT. SCHOOL - DAY   153

Marcus trudges up towards school.

OMIT

OMIT

154   INT. CLASSROOM - DAY   154

Marcus sits in math class.

                    TEACHER
          If z equals seventeen, does x have
          to be more than two? Marcus?

Marcus looks up. He has no idea. A few of his classmates
giggle.

                    MARCUS (V.O.)
          I didn't know what the answer was.
          I didn't know what x equalled, and
          I didn't know how to help Mum.

OMIT

155   INT. SCHOOL HALLWAY - DAY   155

Marcus walks past a sign for the SCHOOL ROCK CONCERT, called
"KIDZ ROCK!" There's a sign-up sheet, and various cool acts
are already listed -- a breakdance crew, a rapper, etc.

                    MARCUS (V.O.)
          And then I realized. There was
          something she said I could do for
          her.

There is a SIGN-UP SHEET on the poster. SHOW YOUR TALENT! it reads. Marcus stares at it.

OMIT

156   EXT . SCHOOL - ENTRANCE - DAY   156

Ellie walks out of school with her usual entourage -- her friends ZOE and SPIKE.

                    MARCUS
          Ellie!

                    ELLIE
          Marcus? Wotcha! Are you stalking
          me?

                    MARCUS
          No.

                    ELLIE
          Too bad. Would've made me feel
          like a celebrity.

                    MARCUS
          I'm thinking of singing at the
          school concert.

                    ELLIE
          You? At the rock concert. Good
          luck.

                    MARCUS
          Thanks. Will you play guitar? All
          I've got is a tambourine.

                    ELLIE
          Are you joking?
            (stops herself)
          Of course you're not. Marcus...I
          don't think it'll go over very big
          with the kids. I mean like they'll
          crucify you.

                    MARCUS
          I don't care about them. It's not
          for them.

                    ELLIE
          Good on ya, Marcus. Tell them to
          shove it right up their arses.

                         MARCUS
          So will you do it? Will you
          accompany me?

                         ELLIE
          Marcus...no. I'm sorry. It's
          suicide.

Ellie walks off, leaving Marcus there.

OMIT

157   INT. SCHOOL CORRIDOR -DAY   157

Marcus takes a deep breath, and picks up a pen.

                         MARCUS (V.O.)
          Mum had said that when I sang, it
          brought sunshine and happiness into
          her life. So I'd do it. Even if it
          meant mine was over.

We see Marcus sign his name, and then under "ACT", the word
"SINGING".

158   INT. FIONA'S HOUSE - DINING ROOM   158

Marcus hands an invitation to the school concert to Fiona,
who takes it and looks at it.

159   INT. STEREO STORE - DAY   159

                         WILL (V.O.)
          My life is made up of units of
          time. Buying a stereo...two units.

Will is looking at a bunch of high-tech stereos. He stands
before a particularly slick model. His face is blank.

160   INT. TRENDY RESTAURANT - DAY   160

                         WILL (V.O.)
          Eating lunch...three units.

Will sits eating lunch on his own, as waiters mill around the
full restaurant.

A CUTE WAITRESS smiles at Will. He doesn't respond.

161   INT. WILL'S FLAT - NIGHT   161

Will goes to his bookshelf. Pulls out a book.

> WILL (V.O.)
> *...Reading...*

Will reads Marcus' gift: <u>The Single Parents Handbook</u>.

> WILL (V.O.) (CONT'D)
> *Two units...*

162   INT. WILL'S FLAT - DAY   162

> WILL (V.O.)
> *All in all, I had a very full life.*

From DIRECTLY ABOVE, we see Will moving around his flat like a rat in a maze.

163   INT. GROCERY STORE - DAY   163

Will drinks coffee alone.

164   INT. WILL'S FLAT - DAY   164

> WILL (V.O.)
> *It's just that...it didn't mean*
> *anything.*

Will puts a CD into the stereo. It reads "One Hit Wonders."

SANTA'S SUPER SLEIGH comes on. Will sits down on the floor, in front of the stereo, and listens to it.

> WILL (V.O.) (CONT'D)
> *The fact was...*

Will kneels forward, his face on the floor.

> WILL (V.O.) (CONT'D)
> *There was only one thing that meant*
> *something to me.*

There's a ring on the DOORBELL. Will gets up, and answers it.

165   EXT. WILL'S FLAT - DAY   165

It's not Marcus. Just a couple of EVANGELICAL TYPES.

> EVANGELICAL TYPE
> Hello sir, have you been saved?

> WILL
> (confused)
> What?

                    EVANGELICAL TYPE
               Have you accepted the --

                         WILL
                    Excuse me.

Will hands the evangelists his remote control, pushes past
them and hurries out of his flat.

166   INT. WILL'S CAR - DAY   166

Will zooms along, the engine whining.

                         WILL (V.O.)
                    Right now, Marcus was the only
                    thing that meant something to me.
                    And Fiona was the only thing that
                    meant something to Marcus. And she
                    was about to fall off the edge.

167   EXT. FIONA'S FLAT - DAY   167

Will rings the bell, and the door opens, revealing Fiona,
with a GUN to her head.

                         FIONA
                    You're too late, Will.

Will closes his eyes as we hear a BOOM -- but then we reveal
that this has just been his nightmarish daydream --

168   EXT. FIONA'S FLAT - DAY   168

Will stands ringing Marcus' doorbell. No response. He looks
up at her window to try to see inside...then sees the sticker
for SPAT in amongst the labour and Greenpeace placards.

                         WILL
                    ...Friday, two o'clock...

169   INT. SPAT MEETING - DAY   169

The SPAT meeting is at the handholding/chanting part of the
event. Fiona is amongst them.

                    SPAT MEMBERS
               SINGLE PARENTS ALONE TOGETHER!
               SINGLE PARENTS ALONE TOGETHER!
                    (MORE)

                    SPAT MEMEBERS
               SINGLE PARENTS ALONE TOGETHER! ALL
               FOR ONE AND ONE FOR ALL!

                    WILL
               (relieved)
     Fiona!

The assembled group turns around to look at Will.

                    FIONA
     Will?

                    FRANCES
     Will! We haven't seen you for a
     while. How's Ned?

                    WILL
     Who? Oh, Ned. He's a load of
     crap. Doesn't exist.
               (off their looks)
     I made him up.

                    MOIRA
     You made him up?

                    WILL
     Yes. To meet women.

                    CAROLINE
     That's sick.

                    WILL
     Yes.

                    MOIRA
     You bastard.

                    WILL
     Yeah, I know. You can cut my penis
     off later if you like. But right
     now...
               (to Fiona)
     Fiona, could we talk privately,
     please?

                    FIONA
     No, Will. These women deserve the
     truth, for once. Whatever you have
     to say, you can say in front of
     everybody.

                    WILL
     O-kaaayyy...well, in that
     case...please don't try to commit
     suicide again.

Some uncomfortable looks.

>   FIONA
>   Um...maybe we should have a little
>   privacy.

170   INT. SCHOOL - GREEN ROOM - DAY   170

Marcus and Simon stand there amongst the kids getting ready
for the school concert. Simon has a recorder. He is staring
nervously at some sheet music. Marcus does some little vocal
exercises and taps his tambourine on his hip.

A kid with a fake gun and East End gangster attire
approaches.

>   LOCK STOCK KID
>   We're doing a scene from Lock Stock
>   and Two Smoking Barrels. What are
>   you doing?

>   MARCUS
>   (optimistically)
>   Singing.

Lock Stock Kid, along with some other nearby kids, snigger.
Simon looks worried.

MR. CHALMERS, a schoolmaster who is running the show with
precision and a measure of hysteria, pokes his head into the
room.

>   MR. CHALMERS
>   Ladies and gentlemen, twenty
>   minutes! Twenty minutes!

OMIT

171   INT. SPAT - DAY   171

Will and Fiona sit in the kitchen of SPAT. Through the pass-
through into the main hall, we see the business of clearing
up at the end of a session going on.

>   WILL
>   I never realized how good the tea
>   was here.

>   FIONA
>   Are you crazy! That was my private
>   business!

                    WILL
          Well, that's the thing, I mean --
          it's not. Marcus is worried about
          you, and I'm worried about Marcus,
          because Marcus is worried about
          you, and --

                    FIONA
          Will, I don't have any plans to
          commit suicide.

                    WILL
          You don't?

                    FIONA
          Not at the moment, no.

                    WILL
          Great! Great! That is fantastic!

Will impulsively leans over and hugs Fiona, a gesture which
takes her completely by surprise.

                    FIONA
          Will, I'm not attracted to you, you
          know.

                    WILL
          What? Oh! For Christ's sakes, no.
          I mean, absolutely not -- are you
          insane?
               (beat)
          That probably wasn't the best
          choice of words. But...look...the
          whole depression thing. The crying
          in the morning thing...I mean, we
          have to fix that.

                    FIONA
          That's what men think, isn't it?

                    WILL
          What?

                    FIONA
          That unless you've got the answer,
          unless you can say, "Oh, I know
          this bloke in the Essex Road who
          can fix that for you," then there's
          no point bothering.

                    WILL
     That's not true. Well, yes, okay,
     it is true. I'd love to know the
     name of the bloke in the Essex
     Road, because I'm going to be
     useless. Lorena Bobbitt out there
     would be more helpful. (ALT: that
     janitor bloke out there with the
     walleye and the fixed grin would be
     more helpful).

                    FIONA
     You're not useless, Will.
     You're...well, you're here. And
     that matters.

Fiona checks her watch.

                    FIONA (CONT'D)
     Look, do you mind getting a move
     on?

                    WILL
     What do you mean?

                    FIONA
     Marcus is singing at his school
     concert.

                    WILL
     Marcus is singing? At school?

                    FIONA
     He is. It's a pop concert.

Will is aghast.

                    WILL
     Fiona...what is he singing?

172 INT. GREEN ROOM - DAY   172

As Simon tootles away on a recorder, Marcus is practicing --

                    MARCUS
     Killing me softly with his song --

Nearby, some kids snigger. Simon looks nervous.

173 OMIT   173

174 OMIT   174

175   EXT. LONDON STREETS - DAY   175

Will's car races through the street. (SECOND UNIT)

176   INT. WILL'S CAR - SAME   176

                    WILL
          I just hope we're not too late.

                    FIONA
          What do you have against Marcus
          singing? He has a lovely voice!

Will is looking panicky.

                    WILL
          You know that dream where you show
          up at school without any trousers
          on, and the whole school laughs at
          you? Well that's what this is
          going to be for Marcus. But real.
          If he sings <u>that</u> song in front of
          those kids...you can just write him
          off till he reaches university. <u>If</u>
          he reaches university. They're
          going to tear him to shreds.

                    FIONA
          You have no right to prevent him
          from expressing himself!

                    WILL
          Expressing himself? He's not
          expressing himself, he's expressing
          you!

The truth of this is beginning to dawn on Fiona.

                    FIONA
          My God, you're...you're right,
          aren't you.
               (thinks)
          Will...am I a bad mother?

                    WILL
          No, you're not a bad mother.
          You're just a looney.

                    FIONA
               (intense)
          No, I'm a bad mother.
               (MORE)

                    FIONA (cont'd)
        I've let things slide, and I
        haven't been noticing properly, and
        he's a special boy, he's a special
        soul, and I've wounded it!!

                    WILL
        Look, will you shut up? You're
        wounding my soul.

177   OMIT   177

178   OMIT   178

179   OMIT   179

180   INT. BACKSTAGE - DAY   180

        Simon and Marcus look out at the audience, which is FILLING
        UP.

                    SIMON
            ...That's a lot of people.

                    MARCUS
                (nervous)
            ...Yeah...

                    SIMON
        This is suicide, Marcus.

                    MARCUS
            ...I can't see Mum.

        The LIGHTS go ON and OFF, signalling the audience to sit
        down.

181   OMIT   181

182   OMIT   182

183   EXT. SCHOOL - DAY   183

        Will's car screeches to a halt.

                    WILL
            Here -- park it!

        Will jumps out, leaving Fiona behind with the high-tech key.

184   INT. SCHOOL AUDITORIUM - STAGE - DAY   184

        The school concert.

A bunch of kids are doing a choreographed BREAKDANCE to Snoop Doggy Dogg's latest album.

185   OMIT   185

186   INT. AUDIENCE - DAY   186

The AUDIENCE of kids seems really into the hip-hop, the hipper kids bobbing their heads coolly.

187   EXT. SCHOOL - DAY   187

Fiona backs up the car, which STALLS.

188   INT. SCHOOL AUDITORIUM - BACK OF AUDIENCE - DAY   188

Will hurries into the back of the darkened house, brushing by peoples' seats.

                    WILL
          Excuse me. Excuse me.

Someone shushes Will.

                    RACHEL (O.S.)
          Sssshh.

Will turns and sees Rachel standing there. He looks stricken. Rachel looks surprised to see him.

                    WILL
          -- What are you doing here?

                    RACHEL
          That's Ali up there.

Will looks up, and sees Ali among the breakdancing hip-hop kids. Looks back at Rachel.

                    WILL
          The kid's got talent. Excuse me.

Will keeps heading towards the stage.

189   INT. SCHOOL AUDITORIUM - STAGE - DAY   189

The hip-hop crew gives a bow and leaves the stage.

190   INT. SCHOOL AUDITORIUM - BACKSTAGE - DAY   190

The curtains close.

                    MARCUS
          Well done, Ali!

191   INT. SCHOOL AUDITORIUM - STAGE - DAY   191

Mr. Chalmers comes onstage and announces, consulting a cheat
sheet.

                    MR. CHALMERS
          That was the Def Penalty Kru with
          "Murder Fo' Life". Our next big
          act is Marcus Brewer, singing
          Roberta Flack's beloved "Killing Me
          Softly", a personal favorite of
          mine. He'll be accompanied by
          Simon Cosgrove on the guitar.

192   INT. SCHOOL AUDITORIUM - BACK OF AUDIENCE - DAY   192

                    WILL
          Christ, it's too late.

193   INT. SCHOOL AUDITORIUM - BACKSTAGE - DAY   193

Marcus starts towards the stage. Simon freezes.

                    SIMON
          Marcus, I can't do this.

                    MARCUS
          Can't do what?

                    SIMON
          Play this song. That lot's going
          to shit all over us.

Simon takes off his guitar.

                    MARCUS
          ...But...Simon...you said!

                    SIMON
          I'm sorry. Here's your five quid
          back.

Simon gives Marcus some money.

194   INT. SCHOOL AUDITORIUM - STAGE - DAY   194

Mr. Chalmers is looking over at Marcus.

MR. CHALMERS
(to the crowd)
Any moment now.

195   INT. SCHOOL AUDITORIUM - BACK OF AUDIENCE - DAY   195

Fiona comes into the auditorium.

196   INT. SCHOOL AUDITORIUM - BACKSTAGE - DAY   196

-- As Marcus notices her.

MARCUS
Mum.

197   INT. SCHOOL AUDITORIUM - AUDIENCE - DAY   197

The kids are starting to get restless. A few CATCALLS and
some SLOW HAND-CLAPPING are starting.

198   INT. SCHOOL AUDITORIUM - STAGE - DAY   198

Chalmers stands there, gesturing for Marcus to come out.

MR. CHALMERS
(stage whisper)
Come on, Marcus, you Wally!

199   INT. SCHOOL AUDITORIUM - BACKSTAGE   199

Will appears at Marcus's side, looking out at the audience.

WILL
Hello, Marcus.

MARCUS
(surprised)
What are you doing here?

WILL
Well, I heard a rumor that you were
going to commit social suicide, so
I thought I'd drop by.

Mr. Chalmers STAGE WHISPERS to Will.

MR. CHALMERS
Excuse me, what is going on here?

WILL
Nothing. Everything's under
control.

>   MARCUS
> My accompanist left!

>   WILL
> Well then I suggest you cut your
> losses and forget about it.

>   MARCUS
> I can't do that. My mum wants me
> to sing it. It'll make her happy.

>   WILL
> Marcus, nothing you do can make
> your mum happy -- I mean -- not in
> the long term. She has to make
> herself feel better.

>   MR. CHALMERS
> Excuse me, but --

>   WILL
>   (to Mr. Chalmers)
> Shut up, you daft old prat.

The SLOW HAND CLAPPING continues from the audience.

>   WILL (CONT'D)
>   (to Marcus)
> I guess what I'm saying is, you
> have to make yourself happy.

>   MARCUS
> I've tried just making myself
> happy. And she's tried making
> herself happy. But it doesn't
> work. You need other people to
> make you happy.

>   WILL
> But see that's just it. If other
> people can make you happy, then
> they can make you <u>unhappy</u> too, and -
> -

>   MARCUS
>   (cuts him off)
> My Mum likes to hear me sing. And
> I like singing for my Mum. And who
> cares if everybody else doesn't
> like it? They can just...<u>eff off</u>.

Marcus heads out onstage. Will makes a last stab at him, as
though trying to catch somebody going over the ledge...

21.

          WILL
      Marcus, don't...

200   INT. STAGE - DAY (INTERCUT)   200

      -- But it' too late. Marcus heads out there, alone, with
      nothing but a tambourine. There's DERISIVE APPLAUSE from the
      audience, as if to say, "Finally!" Then, Marcus stands
      there, looking a little lost and afraid in front of the huge
      crowd.

      For a moment, there is silence.

                AUDIENCE MEMBER
          Go on, Looney Tunes!

      He's immediately SHUSHED by a teacher, but it provokes
      titters from the rest of the schoolkids.

                ANOTHER KID
               (derisively)
          Gi's a song, then!

201   INT. AUDIENCE - DAY   201

      Fiona, moving forward, freezes when she sees Marcus out
      there.

      Ellie stands at the back of the hall, looking afraid for
      Marcus.

202   INT. STAGE - DAY   202

      More shushing, more laughter. We go TIGHT on MARCUS.

                MARCUS
          This is for my Mum.

      Exasperation from the audience, but some of the Mums in the
      audience are clearly touched. Marcus starts, tentatively.

                MARCUS (CONT'D)
          I HEARD HE SANG A GOOD SONG...I
          HEARD HE HAD A STYLE...

      Some LAUGHTER from the crowd, but also a tiny undercurrent of
      support from the mums.

203   INT. SCHOOL AUDITORIUM - BACK OF AUDIENCE - DAY   203

      Fiona takes this in...

204   INT. SCHOOL AUDITORIUM - STAGE - DAY   204

                    MARCUS
          AND SO I CAME TO SEE HIM TO LISTEN
          FOR A WHILE...AND THERE HE WAS THIS
          YOUNG BOY...A STRANGER TO MY E-
          EYE...

Marcus takes a pause. The LAUGHTER GETS LOUDER, despite the
protests of the teachers -- some of them are even laughing
now.

                    MARCUS (CONT'D)
               (sings)
          KILLING ME SOFTLY WITH HIS
          SONG...TELLING MY LIFE WITH HIS
          WORDS...

We are starting to hear the first outright calls of GET OFF!,
but here's also a smaller, less vocal faction that is trying
to support him; however, at this point Marcus is losing the
battle. But then, in the pause in the middle of the chorus,
we hear a mighty GUITAR CHORD STRUMMED. Marcus looks back
and sees Will, striding on stage as cooly as he can manage.
Marcus takes heart and keeps singing...

                    MARCUS   (CONT'D)
          KILLING ME SOFTLY WITH HIS
          SONG...KILLING ME SOFTLY...WITH
          HIS SONG...TELLING MY WHOLE
          LIFE...WITH HIS WORDS...KILLING ME
          SOFTLY...WITH HIS SONG...

Marcus looks over at Will.

205   INT. SCHOOL AUDITORIUM - AUDIENCE - DAY   205

The audience seems somewhat amazed by this new development.

206   INT. SCHOOL AUDITORIUM - BACK OF AUDIENCE - DAY   206

Fiona sings along.

                    FIONA
               (sincere)
          Killing me softly...with his
          song...

We reveal that Fiona is sitting near Rachel, who looks over
at her, then at the stage, Where Will and Marcus are singing
along together...

                  RACHEL
        (to Fiona)
    Are you...are you by any chance...
    Marcus's mother?

                  FIONA
        (proudly)
    Yes, I am!
        (beat)
    Do you know Marcus?

207   OMIT   207

208   INT. AUDIENCE - DAY   208

A kid laughs at Marcus. Ellie, who's standing next to him, SLUGS HIM IN THE ARM.

                  KID
    Oww!

209   INT. SCHOOL AUDITORIUM - STAGE - DAY   209

Will gives Marcus a look, and then, amazingly...Will STARTS SINGING WITH MARCUS.

              WILL AND MARCUS
    HE SANG AS IF HE KNEW ME, IN ALL
    MY DARK DESPAIR...AND THEN HE
    LOOKED RIGHT THROUGH ME, AS IF I
    WASN'T THERE...BUT HE WAS THERE,
    THIS STRANGER, SINGING CLEAR AND
    STROOOOONG...

(NOTE: THROUGHOUT THIS WE ARE CUTTING BACK TO CROWD REACTIONS)

           WILL AND MARCUS (CONT'D)
    STRUMMING MY PAIN WITH HIS
    FINGERS...TELLING MY LIFE WITH HIS
    WORDS...KILLING ME SOFTLY WITH HIS
    SONG...KILLING ME SOFTLY...WITH HIS
    SONG...

But Will is undeterred, despite the LAUGHTER of the crowd. Now Marcus begins to laugh a little. We push in close on Will as he abandons all self-restraint...and CLOSES HIS EYES.

                  WILL
        (still singing)
    I PRAYED THAT HE WOULD FINISH, BUT
    HE JUST KEPT RIGHT O-ON...

                    MARCUS
          Will? Hello?

                     WILL
                    (V.O)
          So there I was, this young boy,
          killing them softly with my song,
          or rather, being killed, and none
          too softly, singing with my eyes
          closed.

The audience is now getting tired of the whole thing. They
begin to BOO as Will keeps SINGING, OBLIVIOUS TO THE JEERING.

                  WILL (CONT'D)
                    (V.O)
          I was like a small, newborn animal,
          with its throat throbbing and
          exposed. Was I frightened? I was
          petrified. This was definitely not
          island living. I was in some
          strange territory.

Will ENDS, strumming his guitar feverishly. The audience is
mixed between APPLAUSE and OUTRIGHT BOOING.

                    MARCUS
          Can we go now?

                     WILL
          Just a second.
               (to the mic)
          Okay, that was pretty crap. I
          admit it.
               (some laughter from the
                crowd; Will is winning
                over the cynics now)
          But it could get worse. Let me
          show you.
               (beat)
          This one goes out to my Dad.

                  WILL (CONT'D)
          OHHHHH....JUST LEAVE OUT THE MINCE
          PIES, AND A GLASS OF SHERRY, AND
          SANTA WILL VISIT YOU AND LEAVE YOU
          FEELING MERRY...
          HO HO HO, HEY HEY HEY, SANTA'S
          SUPER SLEIGH, OHHHHH SANTA'S SUPER
          SLEIGH...

                    MARCUS (V.O.)
          *Will had gone completely round the
          bend. Frankly, I felt embarrassed
          for him.*

210   INT. SCHOOL AUDITORIUM - BACK OF AUDIENCE   210

Rachel stares up at Will onstage.

211   EXT. MARCUS'S SCHOOL - TWILIGHT   211

Marcus and Fiona walk away from school, other parents and
children piling out of the gate behind them.

                    FIONA
          Marcus...thank you. For the song.
          You were terrific.

                    MARCUS
          You think so?

                    FIONA
          Yeah. As a matter of fact I think
          we should celebrate.

                    MARCUS
          Okay.

                    FIONA
          How about McDonald's?

                    MARCUS
          McDonald's?

                    FIONA
          Yeah.

                    MARCUS
          Thanks, Mum, but it's okay.

                    FIONA
          No, really, I want to go to
          McDonald's.

                    MARCUS
          I'm not really hungry.

                    FIONA
                 (trying too hard)
          C'mon. Are you telling me you
          couldn't murder a Big Mac?

                    MARCUS
               (not believing his ears)
     Mum!

Fiona looks relieved.

                    FIONA
     Okay. Another time.
               (pause)
     Any time. I'll be around a while,
     you know. Even if I do cry every
     now and then.

212   EXT. WILL'S DOOR - DAY   212

Will's doorbell rings. He opens it and turns around
automatically, then does a double-take.

                    WILL
     Hi.

                    RACHEL
     You made a complete arse of
     yourself, you know.

                    WILL
     Yeah.

                    RACHEL
     I enjoyed it.

                    WILL
     I bet.

                    RACHEL
     Especially that part where you
     clapped your hands over your head --
               (demonstrates the rock-and-
                roll gesture)
     and nobody went along with you.

                    WILL
     I kind of thought I was drawing
     fire, you know? Like the worse I
     looked the better Marcus would
     look.

                    RACHEL
     In that case Marcus looked
     fantastic.

                    WILL
          So...you basically came here to
          insult me.

                    RACHEL
          Well, yes. I figure you lied to me
          and made me feel like an idiot,
          so...it was the least I could do.

They stand there a second.

                    WILL
          Okay...well...

                    RACHEL
          So can I come in?

                    WILL
               (flirting now)
          Maybe. I'm kind of busy.

                    RACHEL
          Oh yeah? Doing what?

                    WILL
          Watching Countdown.

                    RACHEL
          Right. Well let me ask you
          something. What would you rather
          do -- watch countdown, or have sex
          with me?

Will stands there.

                                        CUT TO:

213   INT. WILL'S FLAT - DAY   213

We see a TV SCREEN showing an episode of countdown. Then we
see Will watching it. Nobody else appears to be there.

                    WILL (V.O.)
          Every man is an island.

We pull back to reveal Marcus...then CAPTIONS READ TEN MONTHS
LATER.

                    WILL V.O
          The thing is, some men are part of
          island chains. Below the surface
          of the ocean they're actually
          connected.

We pull further back to reveal Ali as Rachel leans over the couch and kisses Will and heads off. Ali look over at them.

                    ALI
          Are you going to marry my mum,
          then?

                    WILL
               (taken aback)
          Dunno.
               (beat; honestly)
          I'm still just hoping she'll keep
          seeing me.

                    MARCUS
          I used to want Will to marry my
          Mum.

                    ALI
          For real?

                    MARCUS
          Yeah. But that was when mum was
          depressed and I was really
          desperate.

                    WILL
          Cheers, mate.

                    FIONA (O.S.)
          Will? How do you use this blender
          thing?

                    WILL
          You don't.

We hear the sound of GEARS GRINDING as something goes badly wrong with a Cuisinart. Will gets up.

                    WILL (CONT'D)
          Oh, for Christ's sake.

                    MARCUS (V.O.)
          I used to think two wasn't enough.
          Now there were loads of people.
          And that was great, mostly.

Ellie pops her head into frame.

                    ELLIE
          Oi! Are you two lazy shitbags
          going to help with the food or
          what?

Ellie heads off, and Ali and Marcus resignedly get up from
the couch.

The boys head over towards Will's dinner table, and we see
that it's laid for Christmas dinner...in Will's style, which
is to say, trendy.

Fiona pours whatever vile concoction she was just brewing up
into the glass of none other than RIGHT-ON PERSON #1, who is
sitting at the table now with Rachel, Will, and Ellie as Ali
and Marcus join them.

>   RIGHT-ON PERSON #1
>   And Pa Pa Lay is still in jail,
>   just for telling jokes.
>   (drinks the concoction)
>   Wow. Delicious. What is it?

>   FIONA
>   Sprouts and nuts.

>   RIGHT-ON PERSON #1
>   Sprouts and nuts. Great.

There's obviously something on between the two of them.

>   FIONA
>   So...how do you know Will?

>   RIGHT-ON PERSON #1
>   Oh, we...volunteered together at
>   Amnesty International.

Fiona looks over at Will, impressed.

>   WILL
>   ⊥ dabble.

>   RIGHT-ON PERSON #1
>   And then he just called me up, out
>   of the blue.

Fiona and Will share a look. Will sits down next to Marcus
and leans in confidentially.

>   WILL
>   So are you and Ellie...you know...

>   MARCUS
>   Nah. She's a bit too unstable.
>   By the way, I do think you and
>   Rachel have a shot. I mean, if you
>   don't screw it up.

                    WILL
          Well, thank you, Doctor Love.

People are settling in to eat.

                    FIONA
          Look, before we eat, I'd like to
          say a few words...

                    MARCUS
          Mum. It's Will's party. He gets to
          give the speech.

                    FIONA
          You're right. Will?

Will looks unwilling, but calls of "speech, speech!" force
his hand. Will starts.

                    WILL
          Seeing all of you here... it
          reminds me of something a very wise
          man once said.
               (pause; in Frankenstein
                voice)
          Alone, bad... friends, gooooood!

Will smiles, but nobody else gets it at all.

                    RACHEL
               (ironically)
          Brilliant.

                    WILL
          Right.

We PULL AWAY as people begin to eat, and the conversation
continues...

                    MARCUS
          *I don't know what Will was so
          stroppy about. All I meant was, I
          don't really think couples are the
          future. You know those human
          pyramids? Where all these people
          stand on each others shoulders?
          That's the model of living I was
          looking at now. It's like this
          thing we were reading at school.
          John Donne. Something about people
          being islands. Or not being
          islands. I forget which. Frankly,
          my idea made more sense.*

STILLS

Carefree London bachelor Will (HUGH GRANT) enjoys being the star of his own life.

Rachel (RACHEL WEISZ), a smart, sophisticated single mom, is uniquely attractive to Will.

Top: Marcus (NICHOLAS HOULT) is a 12-year-old misfit who has no friends until he
  meets Will.

Bottom: Fiona (TONI COLLETTE), a struggling single mom, tries to instill old-fashioned
  hippie values in her son Marcus.

Top: The carefree bachelor Will (HUGH GRANT) does not yearn for fatherhood.

Bottom: Will (HUGH GRANT) is attracted to beautiful, intelligent single mom Rachel (RACHEL WEISZ).

Top: Will (HUGH GRANT) befriends Marcus (NICHOLAS HOULT).

Bottom: Marcus (NICHOLAS HOULT) and his mom Fiona (TONI COLLETTE) often differ in their reactions to Will (HUGH GRANT).

Top: Will (HUGH GRANT) is not in his element at a holiday dinner at Marcus and Fiona's house.

Bottom: Will (HUGH GRANT) falls in love for the first time as he gets to know beautiful single mom Rachel (RACHEL WEISZ).

Top: HUGH GRANT, NICHOLAS HOULT, and directors CHRIS WEITZ and PAUL
   WEITZ.

Bottom: Directors CHRIS WEITZ and PAUL WEITZ.

PRODUCTION NOTES

bout a Boy is about a man—a handsome, rich, shallow, self-absorbed, irresistible cad—and the unexpected relationship he develops with a boy he meets while trying to pick up *another* boy's mother.

Terminally single and ecstatically child-free, Will (Hugh Grant), a trendy, 38-year-old Londoner, spends his days buying new CDs, shopping for designer clothes, and worrying about his Audi Coupe and up-to-the-second hairstyle. Nights, whenever possible, are devoted to beautiful women. *Work? What's that?* Thanks to a ubiquitous Christmas standard written by his dad and recorded by everyone from Elvis to the Muppets, Will doesn't have to work like the rest of the world. The royalties rolling in have enabled him to make a profession—an art, really—out of avoiding responsibility.

A no-strings fling with a single mom turns on the proverbial light bulb over his head: maybe a good place to meet women would be single-parent support groups. And so, posing as a single dad with a fictitious two-year-old, he joins S.P.A.T.— Single Parents, Alone Together. Well on his way to charming a single mom named Suzie (Victoria Smurfit), he inadvertently bonds with a 12-year-old misfit named Marcus (Nicholas Hoult), the latchkey son of Suzie's best friend.

That would be Fiona (Toni Collette), a flaky, eccentric, single, hippie-chick. A good boy, Marcus just wants mom to be happy—because she's literally been suicidal since a recent break-up. Add on the fact that the kids at school won't stop picking on him, and Marcus is under more pressure than any 12-year-old should be.

So Marcus turns to the nearest father figure for help. That would be Will. Though he quickly deduces that Will has lied about being a single dad, Marcus badly needs a friend, and try as he does to resist, Will gradually starts to care about the boy's well-being. As Will plays Pygmalion, treating Marcus to a shopping spree for the hippest sneakers and CDs, Marcus's self-confidence grows. Likewise, thanks to Marcus and Fiona, Will finds himself becoming less self-obsessed, less concerned with being the star of his own meager life.

That's when he meets Rachel (Rachel Weisz), a bright, beautiful single mom with a 12-year-old boy of her own. Will finds himself falling in love—real, undeniable love—for the very first time in his life. But it's complicated—especially when Rachel assumes that Marcus is his son.

Who knew love could be so hard? And what strange forms it can take? And what ridiculous things it can make a man do? It's almost more than Will can bear, especially when he realizes how much he cares about Rachel, Marcus, and even wacky Fiona. And when Will puts himself on the line for his makeshift family—without premeditation or calculation— it's a shock to discover that he has saved not only Marcus and Fiona, but himself.

Universal Pictures and StudioCanal present *About a Boy,* a Tribeca/Working Title production starring Hugh Grant, Toni Collette, Rachel Weisz, and newcomer Nicholas Hoult. Directed by Paul Weitz & Chris Weitz (*American Pie),* *About a Boy* is based on the book by Nick Hornby (*High Fidelity)* with a screenplay by Peter Hedges (*What's Eating Gilbert Grape?)* and Chris Weitz & Paul Weitz. Jane Rosenthal, Robert De Niro, Brad Epstein, Tim Bevan, and Eric Fellner produced *About a Boy.* Nick Hornby and Lynn Harris are the executive producers.

About a Boy's behind-the-camera team includes director of photography Remi Adefarasin (*House of Mirth, Elizabeth),* production designer Jim Clay (*Captain Corelli's Mandolin, Felicia's Journey),* costume designer Joanna Johnston (*Castaway, The Sixth Sense),* and editor Nick Moore (*Notting Hill, The Full Monty).* The film's score is by Badly Drawn Boy (Damon Gough) and includes several new songs by this artist, who won the U.K.'s Mercury Prize for best album of the year 2000.

ABOUT THE PRODUCTION ...

From page to screen... Published in 1998, *About a Boy* was Nick Hornby's third novel after the hugely successful *Fever Pitch* and *High Fidelity,* both of which were made into feature films by Working Title Films. *Boy* sold more than one million copies in the U.K. alone and foreign rights were sold in more than 20 countries. Number one on the U.K. bestseller lists, it also hit number two on the *L.A. Times* bestseller list.

About a Boy shows that low self-esteem is not solely a women's issue, that men can be just as vulnerable when it comes to love and self-understanding. In a beguiling, poignant, often hilarious mix of humor and drama, Hornby brilliantly reveals the complex emotional lives of his attractive, eccentric characters as they struggle with issues of isolation, fear of commitment, and the true meaning of love and family in today's urban world.

Tribeca Productions, the New-York based production company headed by Robert De Niro and Jane Rosenthal, recognized the potential of Hornby's novel and optioned the rights in 1998 just prior to publication. "Nick Hornby has such an extraordinary voice," said producer Jane Rosenthal. "It was a natural book to turn into a movie. There aren't many writers who write with that vision in a way that can so easily be adapted for the screen."

Hoping to stay true to the book's unique London feel and atmosphere, Tribeca was looking for a British producing partner. It was a natural progression to team up with Working Title Films, which had already produced the film adaptation of Nick Hornby's *High Fidelity*. Working Title also had a long-standing relationship with Hugh Grant, who had starred in three of their most successful films, *Four Weddings and a Funeral*, *Notting Hill*, and *Bridget Jones's Diary*. "Our partners at Working Title have been extraordinary to work with and have really eased us into shooting in a foreign location," said Rosenthal. "It's been wonderful working with them and I hope to do a lot more there."

Directors of the teen blockbuster hit *American Pie*, Paul Weitz and Chris Weitz may have seemed an unusual choice to direct *About a Boy*, but as Rosenthal pointed out, "They were passionate about the material and passion speaks volumes. In spite of the fact that they are not known for this kind of material, when you get to know them, you understand that this is actually closer to their heart than anything else they have done."

In fact, Chris had read the book on vacation some two years before they became involved and had fallen in love with it. "It was just so immensely charming and fascinating," he said. After convincing his brother Paul that they should buy the film rights, they discovered that the book had already been optioned—and was being set up with another director. That didn't stop them from expressing their enthusiasm to Tribeca—just in case the situation should change. As luck would have it, it did. "We had circled round the project like vultures for a couple of years and finally got our shot at it," said Chris.

"The comedy of this novel is so much more articulate than most comedies these days," said Paul. Having had a huge hit with a teen comedy, he and Chris were keen to tackle a more adult piece. Hornby's pitch perfect dialogue was one of the main attractions. "The only difficulty in adapting the book for the screen," said Chris, "was figuring out, amongst all the rich dialogue, which bits to leave out in order to make it fit into a two hour movie." The other big challenge was balancing Hornby's trademark blend of comedy and drama.

"In any comedy," said Chris, "it's a delicate walk between what is amusing about human foibles and what is disturbing about the way people behave. Finding the right tone was our main assignment."

Working Title's Eric Fellner was intrigued by their perspective. "It was exciting to bring an American point of view to a very British idea and see where they would go with it," noted Fellner.

Keeping the book's London location and ambience was never questioned, especially for Chris, who was schooled at St Paul's, London and Cambridge University.

Casting Will... Hugh Grant had been attached to star before the Weitzes came on board. He had been a huge fan of the book and had also considered buying the rights for Simian, his own production company. Tribeca was thrilled to discover that Grant wanted to play the role of Will and he was signed at a very early stage in the project's development.

Grant was initially surprised when he learned of the Weitzes' interest in the project. "I thought the idea was either insane or so insane it might just be brilliant," he said. "No one loved *American Pie* more than me, but this film was clearly quite a different beast. As it turned out, the idea was in fact brilliant—the Weitzes have many strings to their bow, and although capable of fabulous infantilism, they're also extremely serious and learned people."

As for working with two directors, Grant thought it could be a recipe for disaster: "I have a brother and the idea of directing a film together is unthinkable. There would be blood on the floor before lunchtime. But these two are spookily nice to each other. On the surface, at least." Grant worked very closely with Paul and Chris on the development of the script and the directors acknowledge that this early involvement benefited them all greatly.

The character of Will allows Grant to embrace other elements of his character—as he did so successfully in *Bridget Jones's Diary*—and move further still from the sweet-natured romantic heroes for which he has become so well-known. Will is a 38-year-old slacker, commitment-phobic, low on ambition, and short on self-reflection. Living off the royalties from a Christmas jingle his father wrote many years ago, he enjoys a life of leisure hanging out at fashionable coffee bars and restaurants, watching game shows, and serially dating women. But this life of leisure seems to have turned a little sour by the time he gets to his late thirties when he falls into an unlikely friendship with a 12-year-old boy. The story focuses on the friendship and how they change each other for the better.

There were several elements that made the role attractive to Grant: "The whole thing was right up my alley—very strong source material that was funny and sad and set in England. I also identified quite strongly with one or two aspects of Will."

In spite of some very comic scenes and dialogue, the circumstances of the central characters are difficult. As Grant commented, "I have a feeling that all the best comedy arises out of pain. And there's plenty of pain in this story—particularly in terms of the boy. I personally think Marcus is the best thing Nick Hornby ever wrote."

Fellner said, "Every time we work with Hugh, we see something new. This is a more serious role given the underlying themes of the film, but laced with the comedy, which we know he can do. I think people will be surprised. He really shows what a great actor he is. Hugh is very serious about his work and very committed. He spends an awful lot of time working the scene in his head and he has to be absolutely 100 percent sure that the dialogue is true to the character and the character is true to the story. In addition he is incredibly adept in bringing new material to each scene or each piece of dialogue if it needs it. He never fails to impress us."

Chris Weitz agreed. "Hugh has an extraordinary work ethic. When you see his work, it seems very casual and off the cuff," he observed, "but he does a great deal of work to make it seem that way."

Costume designer Joanna Johnston completed Grant's transformation into trendy urbanite by putting together a wardrobe from designers including Fake, Paul and Joe, Joseph, Diesel, Spiewak, Vexed Generation, and Acupuncture.

Working with children... Tribeca had started searching for Marcus very early, well aware that it could take some time to find the right boy. "We wanted a child who would be accessible and with whom the audience would fall in love," said Rosenthal. "He also had to be a bit quirky, but with a magical presence."

Marcus is an awkward 12-year-old. Between home and school he is miserable. He is bullied at school because he does not conform. He is very protective of Fiona, his hippie vegetarian mother, who encourages him to be different. Marcus is made unhappier by Fiona's depression and recent attempt at suicide. Will could not be less ideal as a father figure, but Marcus decides to make him one. And as it turns out, Will is a perfect friend for Marcus, who needs to learn how to be a 12-year-old, and Marcus is perfect for Will, who needs to gain some substance to his life.

Cast from hundreds, Nicholas was everyone's choice to play Marcus.

"He is incredibly natural and honest in front of the camera," said Paul Weitz. Both directors acknowledged the risk in choosing Nicholas whose previous experience included a handful of small television roles. But, said Chris, "Every day it became more and more clear that he was the right boy and I just thank my lucky stars that we chose him. He is so natural, so organic, that he cannot play a false moment. Everything is just honest and simple."

"He has an incredible power of concentration and cares about his performance," added Paul.

Grant had not worked, at least to this extent, with a child before and somewhat dreaded the prospect. During the auditions, in which he was very involved, he noticed that the kids lost interest after a take or two. "Even I last for three before I get bored," said the actor, "but Nicholas was different. He is so focused and grown-up about the art. He knows his lines and has immaculate instincts." Grant, who sometimes brings new material into a scene as he plays it, was impressed by his young colleague's ability to adapt. "Nicholas would always go along with me and quite often—rather to my annoyance—top my line."

Concluded Fellner: "Nicholas has done an amazing job".

For Nicholas, the chance to play Marcus was a dream come true. He enjoyed learning about everyone else's roles and revelled in being on set so much that his mother who chaperoned him had to literally drag him away at the end of a day's shoot. Cast and crew were impressed that in spite of long working hours he was always focused and always on time. When the directors announced it was a wrap for Nicholas, he cried because he was so upset the experience had come to an end. It took a PlayStation 2 given to him by the filmmakers for a job enormously well done to stop the tears.

Nicholas was thrilled to work with Grant. "He helped me a lot by giving me ideas and teaching me something new every day. At first, I think I was quite rigid but he has made me more natural." The young actor also gave high marks to the Weitzes: "Working with two directors is better than one because they have double the number of ideas."

The leading ladies... With the males in place, it was time to turn attention to the ladies. For the role of Fiona, it was important to have an actress who would bring humor to what is essentially a sad character.

"Toni Collette is really, really funny," said Paul Weitz. "We had all seen *Muriel's Wedding*, in which she plays such a poignant character, but where she is also hilarious. It's hard to find an actress who is so honest with her emotions—and with great comic timing."

Collette savored the chance to play Fiona. "The role is complex and the story moves me," she said. "It takes the knowledge and sheer guts of this kid to make two people who are so set in their ways lean a little closer towards each other and start to compromise a bit." She immensely enjoyed working with her co-stars, and said of Hoult: "He is gorgeous and it's amazing to watch him grow. Kids are closer to some kind of truth because they are less impressed by the ways of the world. Nicholas is very special."

One of the strengths of *About a Boy* is its refusal to head in obvious, sentimental directions. Though there are plenty of opportunities for Will to hook up with Fiona, author Nick Hornby chose a more realistic path, which explores and celebrates the notion of the extended family. Will's romantic interest, in fact, comes completely out of left field.

The filmmakers knew that the actress playing Rachel had to be very strong, not only because she comes into the film halfway through, but also because the audience has to completely understand why Will falls head over heels. Rachel Weisz brings beauty, energy, and an edge of quirkiness, which the filmmakers considered essential to prevent the story from slipping into clichéd territory. "Rachel is magnetic on screen," said Paul Weitz. "The moment you see her, you understand why Will falls in love. But there is also depth to her characterization."

Weisz relished the opportunity to play comedy—and a woman who is fundamentally her own person. "I thought she was a funny character, a bit unruly, a bit unusual," said Weisz, "not just the nice girl who ends up with the boy at the end of the movie."

Shooting in London... Starting in Clerkenwell in North London in April 2001, cast and crew spent seven weeks on location. Clerkenwell offers a less romanticized, more contemporary view of London than movie audiences usually get. "Apart from the mix of old and new, Clerkenwell hasn't been used much as a London film location," said co-producer Nicky Kentish Barnes, "so we are contributing something new." According to production designer Jim Clay, "This is a different London, a real London. London is a vibrant and fabulous place to live, and that was the world we wanted to put in the movie, rather than the traditionally perceived world of old London town."

Other locations included Kentish Town in North London and Notting Hill in West London—for the homes of Fiona and Rachel, respectively—as well as Regent's Park and London Zoo. Chris and Paul Weitz inadvertently provided some on-set entertainment during the shoot, with the increasing number of push-ups they challenged each other to between camera reloads, even on rainy location days.

After seven weeks on location, the production moved to Shepperton Studios to shoot the interior sequences at Will's apartment and Fiona's house. Will's apartment embodies the essence of modern bachelor living. Contemporary and urban, the single-living space is filled with stylish furniture and trendy gadgets, giving a sense that Will has surrounded himself with things to fill his emotional gaps. It's a dramatic contrast to Fiona's house, which is traditional and homey. With fading wallpaper and shabby furniture, her abode is a bit dingy, but nonetheless warm and cozy. Leftist posters are stuck on the windows while vegetarian cookbooks and ethnic totems clutter the living space, leaving no doubt about Fiona's hippie persuasion.

The end... "I think the heart of the film lies in the strong mix of comedy and emotion," said Paul Weitz. "It's extremely funny, but tackles very profound themes about isolation, about family, and about love."

And speaking of love, to give the Weitz brothers a quintessentially British experience, not to mention a big send-off, the producers organized a farewell cricket game at Roehampton. Male cast and crew members had practiced their game during shooting breaks for weeks. One team was captained by Hugh Grant, dazzling in his cricket whites and an able player despite suffering from a bad back. Chris and Paul played on opposing teams with equal success. The sun shone, delicious food was served, and everyone enjoyed their last day together before reluctantly going their separate ways.

CAST AND CREW CREDITS

UNIVERSAL PICTURES and STUDIOCANAL Present a TRIBECA/WORKING TITLE Production

a PAUL WEITZ and CHRIS WEITZ FILM

HUGH GRANT   TONI COLLETTE   RACHEL WEISZ

ABOUT A BOY

ISABEL BROOK   SHARON SMALL   VICTORIA SMURFIT

and introducing NICHOLAS HOULT as Marcus

Casting by PRISCILLA JOHN	*Production Designer* JIM CLAY	*Produced by* JANE ROSENTHAL ROBERT DE NIRO BRAD EPSTEIN
Make-Up & Hair Designer GRAHAM JOHNSTON	*Director of Photography* REMI ADEFARASIN B.S.C.	
Music by BADLY DRAWN BOY	*Executive Producers* NICK HORNBY LYNN HARRIS	*Produced by* TIM BEVAN ERIC FELLNER
Music Supervisor NICK ANGEL	*Co-Produced By* NICKY KENTISH BARNES	*Screenplay by* PETER HEDGES *and*
Original Score Produced By STEVE McLAUGHLIN	*Co-Producers* DEBRA HAYWARD	CHRIS WEITZ & PAUL WEITZ
Costume Designer JOANNA JOHNSTON	LIZA CHASIN HARDY JUSTICE	*Directed by* PAUL WEITZ *and* CHRIS WEITZ
Editor NICK MOORE	*Based on the book by* NICK HORNBY	

CAST

(In Order of Appearance)

Will	Hugh Grant	Lee, The Bully	Ben Ridgeway
Marcus	Nicholas Hoult	Lee's Sidekick	Jack Warren
Christine	Sharon Small	Maitre D'	Russell Barr
Imogen	Madison Cook	Angie	Isabel Brook
	Jordan Cook	Angie's kid	Orlando Thor Newman
John	Nicholas Hutchison	Bitter Ex-Girlfriends	Paulette Williams
Barney	Ryan Speechley		Fritha Goodey
	Joseph Speechley		Susannah Doyle
Fiona	Toni Collette		Delma Walsh
Ellie	Nat Gastiain Tena	Mark	Jonathan Franklin
Ellie's Friends	Laura Kennington	Nicky	John Kamal
	Tanika Swaby	Class Teacher	Tessa Vale
	Peter McNicholl	Woman in Supermarket	Lorna Dallison
	Christopher Webster	Child in supermarket	Bethany Muir

Husband in supermarket	. . . .	Bruce Alexander
Moira/SPAT	. . . .	Joyce Henderson
Frances/SPAT	. . . .	Jenny Galloway
Caroline/SPAT	. . . .	Janine Duvitski
Additional SPAT Women	. . . .	Sue Hyams
		Maggie Kahal
		Lynn Askew
		Beverly Milward
		Danielle Harvey
		Anna Maria Credenzone Philip
		Sarah King
		Susan Ghamsary
		Edna Johnson
Suzie	. . . .	Victoria Smurfit
Mothercare Shop Assistant	. . . .	Frog Stone
Family in Mothercare Car Park	. . . .	Buddy Hunter
		Kristine Perrin
		Nathan Perrin-Hunter
		Rachael Perrin-Hunter
Suzie's Baby Megan	. . . .	Amy Craven
		Rebecca Craven
Park Keeper	. . . .	Sidney Livingstone
Nurse	. . . .	Cathy Murphy
Hairdresser	. . . .	Joanne Petitt
Tom/Amnesty International Worker	. . . . . .	Jason Salkey
Amnesty International Workers	. . . . .	Annabelle Apsion
		Matt Wilkinson
Will's Dad	. . . .	Peter Roy
Candy Throwers	. . . .	Matthew Thomas
		Aaron Keeling
		Scott Charles
Skechers Shopgirl	. . . .	Claire Harman
Cute Waitress	. . . .	Sian Martin
Clive	. . . .	Mark Drewry
Lindsey	. . . .	Denise Stephenson
Lindsey's Mum	. . . .	Rosalind Knight
Rachel	. . . .	Rachel Weisz
New Year's Eve Party Guest	. . . . .	Murray Lachlan Young
Ali	. . . .	Augustus Prew
Simon Cosgrove	. . . .	Alex Kew
Math Teacher	. . . .	Mark Heap
Def Penalty Kru	. . . .	Sunanda Biswas
		James Marshall-Gunn
		Jamie Mayer
		Korede Obashju
Mr. Chalmers, The MC	. . . .	Roger Brierley
Apple Thrower	. . . .	Steffan Pejic
Production Manager	. . . .	Bernard Bellew
First Assistant Director	. . . .	Chris Newman

"A" Camera Operator/Steadicam	. . . .	Peter Robertson
Supervising Art Director	. . . .	Rod McLean
Sound Mixer	. . . .	Tony Dawe
Location Supervisor	. . . .	David Pinnington
Production Accountant	. . . .	Neil Chaplin
Script Supervisor	. . . .	Nikki Clapp
Post Production Supervisor	. . . .	Graham Stumpf

for Working Title

Chief Operating Officer	. . . .	Angela Morrison
Executive in Charge of Production	. . . .	Michelle Wright
Production Executive	. . . .	Sarah-Jane Wright
Head of Legal & Business Affairs	. . . .	Sara Curran
Vice President, Legal & Business Affairs	. . . .	Sheeraz Shah
Chief Financial Officer	. . . .	Shefali Ghosh
Assistant to Eric Fellner	. . . .	Aliza James
Assistant to Tim Bevan	. . . .	Callum Metcalfe
Legal Advisor	. . . .	Lucy Wainwright
Production Assistant	. . . .	Emily Stewart
Production Coordinator	. . . .	Ann Lynch
Second Assistant Director	. . . .	Ben Howarth
Third Assistant Director	. . . .	Alex Oakley
Floor Runner	. . . .	Dathi Sveinbjarnarson
Assistant Coordinator	. . . .	Manuela Cripps
Weitz Brothers Production Executive	. . . . . .	Matt Eddy
Focus Puller	. . . .	David Cozens
Loader	. . . .	Rene Adefarasin
Key Grip	. . . .	John Arnold
Video Assist Operator	. . . .	Chris Warren
Camera Trainee	. . . .	Charlie Grainger
Boom Operator	. . . .	Jaya Bishop
Sound Assistant	. . . .	Christian Bourne
Video Assistant	. . . .	Keziah Barton Whyte
Assistant Accountant	. . . .	Emma Short
Accounts Assistant	. . . .	Jason Potter
Post Production Accountant	. . . .	Tarn Harper
Post Production Accountant's Assistant	. . . . .	Polly Wilby
US Post Production Accounting	. . . .	
		R. C. Baral & Company, Inc.
		Paul Cafferty
		Renee Ryel
Location Manager	. . . .	Steve Hart
Unit Manager	. . . .	Lucy Williams
Location Assistant	. . . .	Kevin Early
Casting Assistant	. . . .	Laura Dickens

First Assistant Editor	Simon Cozens	Fish Animal Handler	Wayne Docksey
First Avid Assistant Editor	Mike Jackson	Duck Animal Handler	Animal Ark
UK Avid Assistant Editor	Tania Clarke		
Second Assistant Editors	Paul Clegg	Food Stylist	Katharine Tidy
	Julian Andraus		
Apprentice Editor	Brock Stoneham	Script Clearance	Ruth Halliday
Editing Department Trainee	David Wheal	Product Placement Manager	Kellie Belle
Post Production Coordinator	Sara Lineberger		
		Construction Manager	John Bohan
Supervising Sound Editor	Richard LeGrand Jr.	HOD Carpenter	Eamon McLoughlin
		Supervising Stagehand	David Jones
Sound Editors	Gary Gerlich	Chargehand Carpenter	Robert Wishart
	William Hooper	Carpenters	Peter Duffy
	Patrick O'Sullivan		Joseph Alley
Dialogue Editor	Walter Spencer		Nicholas Goodall
ADR Supervisor	Robert McNabb		Daryl Carter
ADR Editor	Norval Crutcher, III	Stand-By Carpenters	David Williamson
Assistant Sound Editor	Samuel Webb		Paul Duff
Apprentice Sound Editor	Lee Gilmore	HOD Painter	Clive Ward
Foley Editor	Marilyn Graf	Stagehand	Roy Biggs
		Wood Machinist	Stephen Weston
Supervising Music Editor	Charles Martin Inouye	Painters	Robert Harper
			Jeff Sullivan
Re-recording Mixers	Andy Koyama		Harry Alley
	Chris Carpenter	Stand-By Painter	John Cloke
		Scenic Painters	Michael Finlay
Make-Up Artists	Lorna McGowan		David Haberfield
	Carmel Jackson	Stand-By Stagehand	Len Serpent
Ms. Weisz' Make-Up	Katya Thomas		
		Lighting Gaffer	Jimmy Wilson
Assistant Costume Designer	Guy Speranza	Best Boy	Ian Franklin
Costume Supervisor	Claire Finlay	Generator Operator	Danny Young
Key Set Costume	Helen Mattocks	Electricians	Jamie Mills
Costume Assistants	Martin Chitty		David Moss
	Louise Egan	HOD Rigger	Peter Hawkins
Costume Department Runner	Devina Artley	Rigging Gaffer	Barrie More
		Rigging Electricians	Dennis Holiday
Art Director	Gary Freeman		David 'Jim' Wall
Assistant Art Director	Rosie Hardwick	Stand-By Rigger	Sean Young
Draughts Person	Heidi Gibb		
Art Department Graphics	Jules Faiers	Assistant to Hugh Grant	Sara Woodhatch
Art Department Assistant	Richard Ward	Production Runner	Paul Monaghan
Set Decorator	John Bush	UK Liaison to the Weitz Brothers	Richard Cain
Drapes	Chris Seddon	Assistant to Jane Rosenthal	Meghan Lyvers
Production Buyers	Harriet Orman	Set Intern	Michael Gaster
	Mike Standish		
Property Master	Barry Gibbs	Voice & Dialogue Coach	Jill McCullough
Storeman	Darryl Patterson	Guitar Teacher/On-Set Music Advisor	Paul Englishby
Dressing Props	Kevin Wheeler	Piano Teacher	Rob Nash
	John Botton		
Dressing Props (Chargehand)	Roy Chapman	Tutors	Joy Pollard
Chargehand Stand-By Props	Bill Hargreaves		Steve Fletcher
Stand-By Props	Barry Arnold	Chaperone	Glenis Hoult

Special Effects . . . . Dark Side Effects	Floor Runners . . . . Tom Glaisyer
	Vicki Allen
Stunt Coordinator . . . . Graham Crowther	Sam Pollit
Stand-In for Mr. Grant . . . . James Chasey	Re-recording Services and Sound Editorial Design provided
Stand-In for Nicholas Hoult . . . . Jack Steed	by Universal Studios Sound
Stand-In for Toni Collette . . . . Pauline Gill	Recordist . . . . Bill Meadows
	ADR Recorded at . . . . Future Post London
Unit Publicist . . . . Stacy Mann	ADR Mixer . . . . Ted Swanscott
Stills Photographer . . . . Laurie Sparham	ADR Recordist. . . . . Colin Cooper
	ADR Voice Casting. . . . . Brendan Donnison, M. P. S. E.
Health & Safety. . . . . Paul Jackson	Vanessa Baker
Nurse . . . . Caroline Oxley - McLeod	Foley. . . . . One Step Up
Unit Drivers . . . . Peter Devlin	Main Titles by . . . . The Picture Mill
Ronald Narduzzo	Digital Opticals and End Credits by . . . . . . Pacific Title
Terry Reece	
Eric Francks	UK Editing Facilities . . . . Midnight Transfer
Jason Vanezis	US Editing Facilities . . Universal Studios Editorial Facilities
Camera Truck Driver . . . . Andre Cooper	Editing Equipment . . . . Pivotal Post
Costume Department Driver . . . . Mike Ward	Atomic Film Company, Inc.
Minibus Drivers . . . . Jimmy Batchelor	
Ian Drinkwater	Insurance . . . . AON/Albert G. Ruben
Make-Up Truck Drivers . . . . Graham Pamment	Cameras & Lenses by . . . . ARRI Media
Kim Worley	Lighting Equipment . . . . Lee Lighting
Dining Bus Driver . . . . Tiny Topping	Dailies Telecine. . . . . Mike Frasers
Facilities Drivers. . . . . Steve Manger	Color Timer . . . . Jim Passon
Peter Gathard	Negative Cutting . . . . . . Theresa Repola Mohammed
Colin Thompson	Dolby Sound Consultant . . . . Bryan Pennington
Gordon Hampton	
Tony Smith	Security . . . . Place Invaders
Steve Boyd	Tex's Rangers
Construction Run Around Driver . . . . Ian Johnson	
Props Run Around Driver . . . . Nigel Williamson	Location Facilities provided by . . . . Willies Wheels
Props Stand-By Driver . . . . Alan Burrows	Facilities HOD . . . . Townley Knott
	Art Department Transport . . . . Lays Transport
Additional Crew	
Focus Pullers . . . . Jay Jay Odedra	Background Artists supplied by . . The Casting Collective Ltd.
Tammo Van Hoorn	Catering . . . . First Unit Caterers
Loaders . . . . John Adefarasin	Craft Services. . . . . Natural Addiction
Sam Barnes	Michael Johnstone
Grips . . . . Andy Edridge	Jo McLaren Clark
Stuart Bunting	
Make-Up Artists . . . . Nora Robertson	Executive in Charge of Film Music for Universal Studios. . .
Laura McIntosh	Kathy Nelson
Location Scouts. . . . . Louise Fernandez	
Phil Clark	Songs Produced by . . . Tom Rothrock and Badly Drawn Boy
Supervising Scenic Artist . . . . Steve Mitchel	Score Arranged and Conducted by . . . . Patrick Seymour
Scenic Artists . . . . Nigel Hughes	Orchestra Contracted by. . . . . Andy Brown
James Hunt	Orchestra Recorded at. . . . . Air Studios, Lyndhurst
	Orchestra Engineer . . . . Jake Jackson
	Score Mixed by . . Steve McLaughlin at North Pole Studio
	Mix Assistant Engineer . . . . Jaime Lunn

"Something To Talk About"
(Gough)
Performed by Badly Drawn Boy
Courtesy of XL Recordings Ltd.

"Rue De Noir"
(Barker)
Performed By The Guy Barker International Quintet
Courtesy of Music House (Int.) Limited

"A Peak You Reach"
(Gough)
Performed by Badly Drawn Boy
Courtesy of XL Recordings Ltd.

"Rainy Days And Mondays"
(Nichols/Williams)
Performed By Alexandra Hill

"Santa's Super Sleigh"
Lyrics and Music By Pete Brewis
Performed by Lindsay Benson

"A Minor Incident"
(Gough)
Performed by Badly Drawn Boy
Courtesy of XL Recordings Ltd.

"Bitches And Friends"
(Rinaldi/Garofalo)
Performed By DJ Rodriguez
Courtesy of IRMA Records

"Killing Me Softly With His Song"
(Gimbel/Fox)
Performed By Toni Collette/Hugh Grant/Nicholas Hoult

"Zoo Station"
(Hewson/Evans/Clayton/Mullen)
Performed By U2
Courtesy of Universal-Island Records Limited

"Walking Out Of Stride"
(Gough)
Performed by Badly Drawn Boy
Courtesy of XL Recordings Ltd.

"Feliz Navidad"
(Feliciano)
Performed By José Feliciano
Courtesy of RCA Records/BMG Entertainment

"Sussex Carol"
Arranged By Sir David Willcocks
Performed By The Cambridge Singers
Courtesy of Collegium Records

"Shake Ya Ass"
(Tyler/Hugo/Williams)
Performed By Mystikal
Courtesy of Zomba Records Ltd.

"Avoidance Learning"
(Hanif/Mangat)
Performed By Dead Relative
Courtesy of Universal-Island Records Limited

"Silent Sigh"
(Gough)
Performed by Badly Drawn Boy
Courtesy of XL Recordings Ltd.

"Above You Below Me"
(Gough)
Performed by Badly Drawn Boy
Courtesy of XL Recordings Ltd.

"SuperThug"
(Williams/Hugo/Santiago/Harry/Stein)
Performed By Noreaga
Courtesy of Tommy Boy Music (UK) Limited

"Donna And Blitzen"
(Gough)
Performed by Badly Drawn Boy
Courtesy of XL Recordings Ltd.

Soundtrack by Badly Drawn Boy on

Scene from "Who Wants To Be A Millionaire?"
Courtesy of Celador Productions

Scenes from "Countdown" Courtesy of Yorkshire TV

Scene from "Xena: Warrior Princess"
Courtesy of Studios USA Television Distribution LLC

Scene from "Pet Rescue" Courtesy of Endemol
Entertainment UK Plc and Channel 4 Television

Scene from "Bride of Frankenstein"
Courtesy of Universal Studios Licensing, Inc.

Scene from "Billy Elliot" Courtesy of Universal Studios
Licensing, Inc.

WITH THANKS TO:

Bill Amberg, Missoni, Diesel Style Lab, Boyd, Prada, John Richmond, Spiewak,

Paul Smith, Top Shop, Fake, Lesley Craze Jewellery, Neil Barrett, Pantherella, TAG Heuer, Skechers USA, Inc – UK, Free Tibet, Bulthaup,

Nakamichi/BBG Distribution Ltd,

Co-ordination Group Publications, National Magazine Company Ltd,

International Press Network, Nylon Gallery, Redferns Agency

Produced in Association with
KALIMA Productions GmbH & Co. KG.

Shot at Shepperton Studios
and on location in London, England

M.P.A.A. No. 38482
LOGO (R)
MOTION PICTURE ASSOCIATION OF AMERICA

ABOUT THE FILMMAKERS

PAUL WEITZ AND CHRIS WEITZ (Directors, Screenplay) co-directed the films *American Pie* and *Down to Earth*. Previously, they collaborated on several screenplays, including *Antz* and *Madeline*, based on the popular children's book. They made their acting debut in the Sundance Film Festival hit, *Chuck and Buck*.

Born in New York, the brothers are third-generation filmmakers. Their grandfather was fabled agent Paul Kohner, who represented legendary filmmakers such as John Huston, Billy Wilder, and Ingmar Bergman, and their parents are fashion designer/writer John Weitz and Oscar-nominated actress Susan Kohner.

Paul Weitz graduated from Wesleyan University with a degree in film. In his last year there, his play *Mango Tea* was produced off-Broadway with Marisa Tomei and Rob Morrow by New York's Ensemble Studio Theatre. EST also produced his next works, *Captive* and *All for One*.

Chris Weitz earned his bachelor's and master's degrees in English literature at Britain's Cambridge University. He went on to work as a journalist for several newspapers in the U.K. and U.S. before starting to work in film with his brother.

PETER HEDGES (Screenplay) is the author of the novels *What's Eating Gilbert Grape* and *An Ocean in Iowa*. His screenplay adaptations include *What's Eating Gilbert Grape* and Jane Hamilton's *A Map of the World*, which starred Sigourney Weaver and Julianne Moore. He is making his directorial debut with his original screenplay, *Pieces of April*, which stars Katie Holmes, Oliver Platt, and Patricia Clarkson. Hedges lives with his wife and two children in Brooklyn, New York.

NICK HORNBY (Executive Producer/Author) was born in 1957 and worked as a teacher before becoming a full-time writer. His first book, *Fever Pitch*, enjoyed huge critical success and became a bestseller. It was short-listed for the NCR Prize and was voted the William Hills Sports Book of the Year in 1992, and the William Hill Sports Book of the Decade in 1995. *Fever Pitch* was adapted for the screen by Hornby and released in March 1997.

Hornby's second novel, *High Fidelity*, was published in the spring of 1995 in the U.K. It won the Writer's Guild Award for fiction in 1996, and was made into a film by Disney.

About a Boy was published in 1998.

Speaking with the Angel was published in January 2000. An anthology of short stories by different writers, Hornby edited and contributed to the collection. All profits were donated to the Tree House Trust, a charity for autistic children that Hornby co-founded.

His latest novel, *How To Be Good*, was published in May 2001 to critical acclaim and continues to ride high on best-seller lists on both sides of the Atlantic.